I0620174

The Stress-Free Guide to Parenting a Child With ADHD

Effective and Proven Strategies for Alleviating Anxiety and Forming Strong Bonds **Without** the Hassle

Regina Michaels

InkRealm Publishing
BRINGING IMAGINATION TO LIFE, ONE PAGE AT A TIME

Table of Contents

Introduction

Why fit in when you were born to stand out? –Dr. Seuss

I used to love family dinners. I've always been close to my family and sharing a meal together has always felt safe and comfortable. It was a place where I could be myself, share my excitement about my latest hobby, or find my peace after a crazy week. I still love my family dearly, don't get me wrong, but lately I've been dreading family dinners. In fact, I've been dreading most social events. It all started when my little boy got diagnosed with ADHD. It's not that my family all of a sudden didn't love and accept him. On the contrary, it's unsolicited advice that drives me into a state of panic. So, as I sat at yet another dinner, biting my tongue almost in half as I listened to another uncle give advice on how to discipline my child, I felt utterly lost.

As a mom, it's my job to protect, nurture, and care for my kids. But that would be a much easier job if every child came with a manual. "When sad, provide comfort for three minutes, then distract them with a snack," or "When overwhelmed, gently hug for five seconds then suggest playing outside." Every child is different, which means that you have to figure it out from scratch every time you start the parenting journey. On top of that, some kids come with additional unique qualities, which in my little guy's case is called ADHD. Usually, I'm pretty good at embracing his unique qualities, biting my tongue when people say things they don't really mean or have no real knowledge about, but other days I get overwhelmed and I feel like a failure. I want to scream at everyone who dares to look at him with a funky look on their face, but I also want to hide away from everyone and everything.

Raising a child is no joke, and raising a child with ADHD can sometimes seem impossible. It was at that dinner, a couple of years ago, that I decided that I wanted to do something about it. Even though I wanted to grab my soap box and start screaming the facts at everyone, I knew that I needed a better plan. That night, after my husband had already fallen fast asleep, I had my eureka moment. "A book!" I screamed, scaring my poor husband into another dimension. "I'm going to write a book to help parents like us," I explained to my husband, and so my research and writing journey began. And here we are.

Hi, my name is Regina Michaels, and I am a mom of two beautiful children. I am also a wife and have to work to make ends meet. I am blessed with a family who cares so much that they sometimes overstep boundaries, but luckily, I'm also blessed with confidence to tell them to back away slowly. Most importantly, I am passionate about helping parents who, like me and my husband, are raising a child, or perhaps children, with ADHD. Do I have all the answers? Not even close! However, I have dedicated many, many hours to researching, testing, and applying tips, tricks, and other wise words that can help you as much as they have helped my family. It's important to know that this book won't change who your child is. Reading a book on ADHD will in no world change your child into a zombie who doesn't act like him or herself anymore. I feel the need to point that out, since it was something I used to be scared of. I didn't want to change my little boy, I simply wanted to help him, his sister, and the rest of our family to understand him. So, rest assured, I'm not in the business of changing your child. In fact, I'm in the business of embracing the unique qualities and abilities of every individual child.

On this journey, we'll dive into various topics regarding ADHD. In fact, we'll start with the very basics of it all: What even is ADHD? We'll look at the medical side of things, as well as the practical side of ADHD, such as how to know if your child has ADHD and how to embrace their neurodiversity. In Chapter 2, we'll explore different parenting styles and strategies that work with ADHD kids. Don't worry, I won't tell you what to do and how to do it, but I'll share with you how to embrace empathy and positivity with your parenting style. Up next, we'll look at establishing effective routines. We'll say goodbye to unnecessary chaos, and hello to routines that your ADHDer will embrace. In Chapter 4, we'll look at effective communication and how to improve your communication and connection with your child, which will lead us right to Chapter 5, which is all about discipline and managing behavior. In the following chapter, we'll explore nurturing emotional well-being and how you can support your little one through the ups and downs that they might experience.

We'll also touch on the subject of academic success, since that is probably a big pain point in your life right now, or at least a point of worry. I'll share with you helpful tools on how to create a tailored work environment for your ADHDer and how to cultivate a love for learning within their minds. Chapter 8 is all about managing transitions and challenges since it can be really challenging for a child with ADHD to adapt to change, making it a tricky situation for all parties involved. In Chapter 9, we'll explore how to help your little one have good social skills and cultivate peer relationships. Finally, we'll look at strengthening the parent-child bond, as well as strengthening family support and parenting as a team.

I know that it sounds like a lot to digest all at once, but let's not get ahead of ourselves. We'll take it one chapter at a time and do the best that we can. After all, parenting a child with ADHD isn't about being the perfect parent all the time, but about constantly showing up for your child. So, well done! You're already showing up, which means you're already one step closer to helping your child navigate the ADHD waters of life. Before we jump in, I want to encourage you to really embrace this journey fully. Whether you think these methods and pieces of advice I'll provide will work or not is irrelevant at this point. Rather, I want to challenge you to give it your all. Jump in and grab on to every piece of advice as if that's the piece that you've needed all this time. Try it all and then decide whether it's working or not. Let your child do the talking as you observe how they respond to new techniques and routines. The words in this book won't help you if they remain only words in this book. You have to take the lessons and implement them practically in order to really see a difference.

My hope and dream is that by the end of this journey you'll feel empowered, at peace, and excited to parent your ADHDer. I trust that you'll gain

- empathy and understanding beyond what you already have.

- practical, research-based strategies research-based.

- an improved relationship with your child.

- positive behavioral changes within your child.

- enhanced academic performance for your child.

- emotional support and coping strategies that you can teach your child as well as other family members.

- creative parenting techniques that will aid you daily.

- family harmony and understanding.

- inspiration and hope for the future.

- community and connection.

- long-term success and that you'll once again enjoy being a parent.

I also want to encourage you by saying well done. I know it's hard; trust me, I get it. But you're not alone.

You're not failing.

You're not a terrible parent.

Your child will be okay, and so will you.

So, buckle up—our ride through the neurodivergent brain is about to begin and you have the VIP seat!

Chapter 1:

Understanding ADHD

Unfortunately, we live in a culture where children with ADHD are often considered as "just being naughty," or "that child that can't sit still in class." But there is much more to ADHD than that. ADHD stands for attention deficit hyperactivity disorder (Hasan, 2018). Despite what many people think or believe, it is a medical condition that goes beyond your behavior or ability to pay attention in class. In fact, someone with ADHD experiences different brain development that someone without ADHD and that's why it affects you in all areas of your life, not just in school. In this chapter, I want to deep dive into the world of ADHD in order to really understand what it is. The best way you can help your child is by having an inside scoop on what is going on in their heads and offering help in a way that will actually be perceived as help. Let's jump in by asking the most important question—What is ADHD?

What Is ADHD?

Firstly, you need to be aware of the fact that not all ADHD is the same. There are different kinds of ADHD that affect children and adults in different ways. While there are similar symptoms, there are also differences that we need to be aware of as parents.

Types of ADHD

ADHD can be divided into three main types:

- **Primarily Inattentive:** While people with primarily inattentive ADHD also experience impulsivity to some extent, they often more commonly experience other symptoms. Inattentive-type ADHD often shows up as missing details or getting easily distracted. You'll also get bored quickly and have trouble focusing on a single task at hand. Children with Inattentive ADHD might have difficulty organizing their thoughts and will often lose their belongings, such as pencils and papers. When you speak to someone with inattentive ADHD, it might come across as if they're not listening to you at all, since they're often caught in their own daydream. Inattentive ADHDers also struggle to process information and will have trouble following directions (Roth & Weiss, 2021).

- **Primarily Hyperactive-Impulsive:** This type of ADHD is characterized by hyperactive behavior. You'll often see them squirming, fidgeting with something, or feeling restless. People with hyperactive-impulsive ADHD will have trouble sitting still and they tend to speak more than your average person. They'll often touch or play with objects even when they know they're not allowed to, like in a museum, for example. This type of ADHD is often described as people who are always on the go and can be quite impatient. Children will often play or act out of turn and not consider the consequences of their actions in the moment. They tend to also blurt out answers and surprises (Roth & Weiss, 2021).

- **Combined:** Combined ADHD means that you don't exclusively fall into one or the other. You might have symptoms of both, but not all the symptoms of one specific type. This is the most common type among children and it can change as they get older (Roth & Weiss, 2021).

The Neurobiology of ADHD

The neurobiology of ADHD is quite complex. Luckily, we're not doctors, so we don't have to understand every single bit of theory. However, there are a couple of things that are worth knowing if you want to truly understand your child better. First, we need to look at dopamine and how it's produced and managed differently when ADHD is part of the ball game.

Dopamine and Norepinephrine Imbalance

The causes of ADHD are unclear, but one thing that is apparent is that the neurotransmitters in the brain play a large role in ADHD. Dopamine and norepinephrine are two types of neurotransmitters that are usually connected to ADHD. The role of dopamine is to regulate emotional responses and motivate you to take action in order to achieve specific rewards. Its main job is to help you feel pleasure and reward. But what happens when dopamine isn't regulated properly? Well, some researchers believe that people with ADHD have different levels of dopamine than those without it (Duggal, 2016). In fact, they have observed that people with ADHD have higher concentrations of proteins, which enable dopamine to be transported. The more proteins, the lower the dopamine levels in the brain. In other words, instead of regulating your emotions in the brain, dopamine travels all through the body. This often results in quick emotional changes or mood swings, one of the many symptoms of ADHD.

Dopamine and norepinephrine aren't the only neurotransmitters that are involved with ADHD, but they both play an essential role. Norepinephrine is in charge of helping you to stay awake and be alert. In other words, without regulated norepinephrine, you'll have a hard time focusing. On top of that, norepinephrine also contributes to your fight or flight response. It helps you to decide when something is a threat you can stand your ground against or when it's better to just run away. Too little norepinephrine will result in struggling to control impulses and difficulty focusing (Watson, 2022). When both dopamine and norepinephrine are not regulated properly, it's a recipe for hyperactivity, lack of focus, and impulsive behavior. Sound familiar?

However, it's not only the neurotransmitters that make the neurobiology of ADHD different than brains without it; there are also both structural and functional differences. Let's have a look.

Brain Structure and Function Differences

Many of the characteristics of ADHD are related to executive functioning. In other words, the way the brain works is different than what someone without ADHD might experience. Executive functions are the skills we all use on a daily basis to function and manage tasks. Several parts of the brain are required to function together in order to manage executive functioning properly, but the most prominent part of the brain required for executive functions is the prefrontal cortex. Over the years, research has found that children with ADHD typically develop their prefrontal cortex slower than other children (Wilkins, 2023). In other words, the physical brain is different than what is considered a normal brain. The cerebellum is also shaped differently in children with ADHD, which means that the way their brains regulate movement is different. However, even though the brain might look different as a child, eventually it catches up and by the time you're an adult, your brain will look the same as any other brain, which is why many children "outgrow" their ADHD to some extent as they get older.

Genetic Factors and Environmental Influences

The cause of ADHD has been debated among scholars for decades. While some firmly believe that it's all about genetics (nature), others believe that it has more to do with your environment (nurture). However, many have come to the conclusion that it is a combination of these two factors that can lead to ADHD. If it was only one or the other, why would one sibling experience ADHD while the other doesn't? However, one thing is clear, and that is that ADHD is a neurodevelopmental disorder, which means that it's something you're born with and not something that develops over time (Marie, 2021). However, even though the environment can't cause ADHD to develop, it plays an essential role in ADHD management, which is why we'll discuss how to create the best environment for your child later on in this journey. For now, all you need to know is that your child didn't develop ADHD because you did something wrong as a parent. So, take a deep breath and let go of that fear you might have been subconsciously harboring.

Now that we have a better understanding of what ADHD is, it's time to look at the signs and symptoms of ADHD. I'm sure if you're here, you either already know that your child has ADHD, or perhaps you're wondering whether that's the case. Looking at these symptoms will help you to identify whether your child might be struggling with ADHD and it will also help you to better understand your child.

Identifying ADHD in Your Child

Although there are many visible symptoms of ADHD, in some children it can be harder to notice than in others. For example, if your child is performing well at school, you might think that it's impossible for them to have ADHD, but that's not the case. ADHD can look different in every person, but there are some common symptoms that you can look out for. For this particular section, we'll look at early signs and symptoms of ADHD in order to help you discover whether your child might be struggling with ADHD or not.

Early Signs and Symptoms

There are three main signs and symptoms of ADHD that can be spotted early on in a child's life: inattentiveness, hyperactivity, and impulsivity (Hasan, 2022).

- **Inattentiveness:** Being inattentive means that you get easily distracted and have trouble focusing on the task at hand. Inattentiveness doesn't necessarily manifest physically. Many children get distracted within their own minds. They might look at you and appear as if they're listening but be in their own world far away from here. If you notice that your child struggles to remember instructions or that they lose track of their things, it can be a sign that they are inattentive. You can also test this by giving them some simple instructions and noticing whether they remember or whether they ask you to repeat the instructions multiple times.

- **Hyperactivity:** Children who are hyperactive will constantly look for something to fidget with. You might also see them bouncing their leg or tapping their foot when they're asked to sit still. Hyperactive children will also get bored very easily and will have trouble sitting still or remaining quiet. You'll often see hyperactive children try new things such as climbing on the couch or jumping from furniture to furniture. They often disrupt others without meaning to, especially other siblings.

- **Impulsivity:** If your child often acts before they think, it might be a sign that they have ADHD. Being impulsive might look different in children than in adults. For children, being impulsive might mean interrupting others while they're speaking, doing things without asking permission, and taking things that aren't theirs to take. They'll find it extremely difficult to wait their turn and they might get emotional when they get reprimanded for their impulsive behavior.

Of course, this isn't an exhaustive list of all the signs and symptoms of ADHD in children, but it's a good start. If you just read through that list and ticked every box for your child, it might be time to take the next step and get your child diagnosed. Even if you've diagnosed your child yourself, it's essential that you get a medical and psychological assessment as well. Why? Well, these symptoms aren't exclusive to ADHD, which means that while you might assume your child has ADHD, they might be struggling with something else. That's why a medical assessment is required. Once the medical assessment is clear, your child can go through a psychological assessment, which will diagnose your child with ADHD if that's the case.

In order to get a diagnosis, you should make an appointment with your doctor and ask them for a check-up. If the check-up is clear, they can refer you to someone that will be able to diagnose your child accordingly. It might help the diagnosis along if you go to the appointment prepared. The doctor might require some information from you, such as (Hasan, 2022)

- whether your child often gets in trouble at school.

- whether your child acts impulsively.

- your child's discipline at home.

- a complete health check to rule out any other possibilities.

Your doctors will also aid you in finding the best treatment plan for your child, which is why it's so essential that you don't only rely on self-diagnosis.

ADHD vs Other Disorders

As I mentioned earlier, some symptoms of ADHD might correspond with symptoms of other disorders. However, it's important to know that ADHD and these other disorders aren't the same thing and therefore, shouldn't be treated as the same. There are a couple of disorders that commonly get confused with ADHD, so let's have a look at what makes ADHD different than these disorders.

Learning Disabilities

Learning disabilities and ADHD are often confused. ADHD isn't a learning disability but it can affect learning. A learning disability is a brain-based disorder that affects your average intelligence (Thenu, 2022). It's not the same as an intellectual disability and it's different from ADHD. Children with a learning disability are just as smart as children without a learning disability, but they process information in a different way. In other words, the information takes the scenic route to get to the brain instead of the highway. A learning disability makes it difficult to acquire or learn a specific skill, such as math or reading. ADHD impacts your global ability to focus and isn't topic-specific (Thenu, 2022).

Let's use the example of three young boys sitting in math class. The first boy has strong executive function and doesn't have ADHD or a learning disability. He listens to the teacher, looks at the example on the board, and then understands the concept. He then proceeds to work on his assignment, taking it one math problem at a time. Boy two suffers from ADHD. He listens to the teacher as she explains the new math concept. As he listens, he notices a bird flying past the classroom. He starts thinking about his pet bird at home and how he can't wait to teach the bird to talk after school. He thinks about home and his favorite TV show that he wants to watch once he is done with his supper. Thinking of supper makes his stomach rumble and he thinks about what he'll get from the cafeteria when it's break time. He looks at the black-board where the teacher is giving examples of the math problem, which he now has no idea how to solve and he feels bored. However, he turns to his friend and asks for help. Eventually, he understands the concept as well.

Boy three has a learning disability. He notices the problem on the board, listens to the teacher, but can't seem to grasp the concept. He isn't distracted or dreaming about anything else, he's not talking to his friends or procrastinating on his assignment on purpose, he's just waiting for the information to sink in. Eventually, he grasps the idea, but the teacher has already moved on to the next subject. As you can see, while both boys two and three might appear to have the same issue (unfinished work), what happened within their minds is completely different. That's why ADHD and learning disabilities shouldn't be considered the same issue.

Autism Spectrum Disorder

Autism and ADHD are both neurodevelopmental disorders, and even though they have several symptoms in common, they are two very different, distinct diagnoses. Of course, in some cases, it's possible to have both autism and ADHD, but that doesn't mean it's the case with everyone.

Before we look at the difference between ADHD and autism, let's first look at the symptoms that they can have in common (Rudy, 2022).

- impulsivity

- lack of focus

- difficulty organizing

- social challenges

- sensory issues

- emotional immaturity

However, even though the symptoms are the same, the reasoning behind the behavior is very different. For example, when it comes to a lack of focus, people with ADHD typically get distracted by external events, while someone with autism will most likely get distracted by their own thoughts. In other cases, even though people with ADHD and with autism might both struggle in social situations, an ADHDer might struggle due to talking over others or having the inability to conform, while someone with autism might struggle due to the inability to read body language or take social cues. While the cause of ADHD is unknown, we know that autism is caused by genetic and environmental factors. When it comes to completing tasks, ADHD individuals might struggle due to getting distracted, while individuals with autism might struggle if they have to interact with others or make use of their communication skills.

Behavioral Disorder

Behavioral disorder is a broad term that refers to any patterns of disruptive behavior. This type of behavior is often considered inappropriate and it can interfere with a person's ability to function at work, school, or in social settings. There are many differences between ADHD and behavioral disorder, especially since there are various types of behavioral disorder, such as oppositional defiant disorder, conduct disorder, and intermittent explosive disorder. They key differences between ADHD and behavioral disorders can be categorized into four groups:

- **Cause**: While the cause of ADHD is unclear, behavioral disorders are caused by a combination of factors such as genetics, brain injury, abuse, and neglect.

- **Symptoms**: ADHD characteristics are more specific to paying attention, hyperactivity, and acting impulsively. On the other hand, behavioral disorders can manifest in a variety of ways, depending on the disorder. People with oppositional defiant disorder (ODD) are often argumentative and defiant, while people with conduct disorder (CD) are extremely aggressive and will behave destructively.

- **Course**: ADHD lasts your entire life, while behavioral disorders can vary in their course, depending on the person. Some experience their disorder only for a short period of time, while for others, it can last a lifetime.

- **Treatment**: ADHD has no cure, but it can be treated with lifestyle changes and medication. On the other hand, behavioral disorders should be treated by professionals, usually in the shape of therapy, since they can cause behaviors that can be dangerous to others.

The biggest difference is that ADHD very rarely, if ever, causes others to be in danger. It affects mostly the person with ADHD, at least physically. On the other hand, people with behavioral disorders can be a danger to others around them when they experience outbursts or breakdowns. When someone with CD gets upset, they might act violently. Even though ADHDers also experience increased emotions, the majority of it is nonviolent and more likely manifests in crying or screaming.

As much as there is a big difference between ADHD and other disorders, ADHD itself can manifest differently in various people. For example, ADHD can look very different in males and females. Let's have a closer look at how it can differ between genders.

The Differences Between Genders

There are a lot of people out there who have ADHD. In fact, according to the Centers for Disease Control and Prevention (CDC), back in 2016, approximately 6.1 million children in the United States had an ADHD diagnosis (Jones, 2022). Not only was that statistic 7 years ago, it also only counted children in the US. Crazy, right? Well, even though so many children are diagnosed with ADHD, it's shocking that so many doctors and researchers fail to mention just how different ADHD can manifest in boys versus in girls. According to that same 2016 statistic, it showed that the diagnosis for boys is much higher than it is for girls, and that's not simply because less girls have it. It's because most of the research has been done on males, so ADHD symptoms that manifest differently in girls are often overlooked. This all can result in girls going undiagnosed their entire lives.

Boys are three times more likely to get diagnosed with ADHD than girls, despite more recent research showing that the ratio for ADHD is very much 50/50 for boys and girls (Jones, 2022). There are a number of reasons why boys are more likely to get diagnosed, so let's have a look.

- Girls are more likely to show inattentive symptoms, meaning they're stuck in their own minds. On the other hand, boys are more likely to show hyperactive symptoms, which are more outward and visible. If you have two children, which one are you more likely to suspect of having ADHD—the one who plays quietly on their own, stuck in their own dreamworld, or the one who quite literally can't even sit still while eating his dinner? Probably the second one, am I right? As you can see, it's not that researchers or doctors are out to get girls by not diagnosing them; it's just easier to diagnose the boys, so it happens more frequently.

- Girls are more likely to find a way to deal with their ADHD on their own. In other words, they develop compensatory adaptive behavior and coping strategies to mask their symptoms. Now, we could go into a whole debate as to why that's the case, but that's a can of worms we'll leave for another day.

- Since most girls have internal presentations of ADHD and not external, they often get misdiagnosed with a different disorder, such as anxiety or depression. In many cases, the anxiety and these other disorders are coexisting, but the ADHD gets overlooked.

In short, girls are less likely to show their ADHD to those around them, while boys act more disruptively, making it more noticeable. Girls who struggle with ADHD often go their entire lives masking it or struggling internally due to a lack of noticeable "red flags." Here's a list of ADHD symptoms and signs that are more likely to manifest in each gender (Jones, 2022).

ADHD in Boys

Since boys with ADHD are often considered the stereotype of what ADHD is, it's important to notice the differences. This will help you to spot ADHD in girls more clearly and not dismiss their symptoms as non-ADHD-related. Boys with ADHD often showcase these signs:

- constant fidgeting

- difficulty staying seated

- climbing on top of and over everything

- always on the go

- inability to do activities quietly

- talking excessively

- blurting out answers and responses even when it's not their turn

- difficulty waiting their turn or waiting in a line

- intruding on others without their permission

- rule-breaking behavior

- frequent arguments with others

ADHD in Girls

While girls can also have the same symptoms and signs as boys do, they are more likely to have ADHD symptoms that are internal and less obvious, such as:

- lack of paying attention to close details

- making mistakes in schoolwork that's often attributed to carelessness

- difficulty staying focused on activities and conversations

- zoning out while in a conversation

- struggling to follow specific instructions

- poor time management and disorganization

- avoiding tasks that require a lot of mental effort

- frequently losing personal belongings

- forgetting common tasks such as doing chores and getting a permission slip signed

As girls get older, ADHD can lead to self-esteem issues or a poor self-image, especially when the ADHD isn't diagnosed. Instead of understanding what makes them different, they feel like a failure or as if they can't do anything correctly. A missed or late diagnosis can also result in depression, eating disorders, and sleep disorders.

Whether your child is a boy or a girl, it's essential that you look at all the signs and symptoms and not fall into the trap of a stereotype. Instead, pay special attention to the small details of their world and try to see things from their perspective. Most importantly, it's essential that you embrace their neurodiversity.

Embracing Neurodiversity

Embracing neurodiversity doesn't mean that you don't try to manage it; it simply means to accept the fact that it is something your child is dealing with, while celebrating the things that make them unique. Here's the fun part—neurodiversity isn't all bad! There are positives to being neurodiverse, but chances are that your child won't feel free to embrace those positives if you don't embrace them first. Embracing neurodiversity involves acknowledging the differences, adjusting to help them better, and not expecting your neurodivergent child to behave like other children. So, let's start embracing our children with ADHD and their unique minds by looking at the positives of neurodiversity.

The Positives

Neurodiversity brings a wealth of positive aspects and it often comes with a strong will to practice problem-solving. They also have fresh perspectives and can often effortlessly see something in an objective light that others might struggle to do. However, there are three positives that I specifically want to bring your attention to: creativity, hyperfocus, and energy.

- **Creativity:** Being more creative than others is common among ADHDers. Being creative is having the ability to generate new and original ideas and it involves many different cognitive skills. People with ADHD often have unique cognitive strengths that are very beneficial to creativity. For example, people with ADHD are often good at divergent thinking, which is the ability to come up with a variety of different ideas. People with ADHD are also often good at seeing the world in new and different ways. This can be helpful for coming up with creative solutions to problems. Some of the most creative people out there are diagnosed with ADHD, such as Jim Carrey, Justin Timberlake, and Will Smith.

- **Hyperfocus:** When someone with ADHD goes into hyperfocus mode, they are in a state of intense concentration. They will focus on the task at hand as if their life depends on it! This can be a negative thing, since it can lead to burnout or poor healthcare, but it's also a great thing because tasks will most definitely get done. Hyperfocus can be a powerful tool for creativity and productivity because when people with ADHD are hyperfocused on something they are interested in, they can become incredibly efficient. They may be able to work for hours on end without getting distracted, and they may produce work of exceptional quality. Hyperfocus is especially beneficial in emergency situations or when they are under a lot of pressure.

- **Energy and Enthusiasm:** Energy and enthusiasm are two positive aspects of ADHD that can be harnessed to achieve great things. People with ADHD often have a boundless supply of energy, which can be channeled into creative pursuits, athletic endeavors, or simply living life to the fullest. If you want someone to support you fiercely, someone with ADHD is a good option, since they will cheer you along wholeheartedly.

When you start to recognize these qualities about your child, you'll start to notice the positive side of ADHD more and more. I know that an ADHD diagnosis at the beginning can be quite scary, but trust me, once you start to embrace it you'll see it as a gift and not something that is "wrong."

Myths and Realities About ADHD

Part of why so many people fear an ADHD diagnosis for their child is because there are many myths and misconceptions about it. There are three myths in particular that always get my blood boiling. So, before I turn into The Hulk at the dinner table, allow me to talk you through these three myths about ADHD and what the truths behind them are.

It's Not a Real Disorder

The myth that ADHD is not a real disorder is inaccurate because there is a significant amount of scientific evidence to support its existence. Saying that ADHD isn't real is like claiming that gravity doesn't exist. Most people who believe that ADHD isn't a real disorder have most likely been offended in the past by a claim that they might have ADHD or they've never experienced an attention problem whatsoever. This myth is often sold as fact by people who are uninformed. However, thanks to genetic, brain imaging, and neurochemical studies, we can rest assured knowing that ADHD is very real and it's not just an imaginary "illness."

They Just Need to Try Harder

Speaking of an imaginary illness, there are many people out there who believe that if you have ADHD, you're simply not trying hard enough to succeed. Struggling to sit still? Try harder. Can't concentrate? Try harder! The myth that people with ADHD just aren't trying hard enough is inaccurate because ADHD is a neurodevelopmental disorder that affects the brain's ability to regulate attention, impulse control, and executive function. People with ADHD are not lazy or unmotivated. They simply have a different way of thinking and behaving. As a result of these challenges, people with ADHD may often struggle in school, work, and social settings. They may also experience low self-esteem and frustration. Saying that someone with ADHD "just isn't trying hard enough" is like telling someone who only has one leg to "just grow another."

It's Only Present in Children

Many people believe that ADHD is only present in children and that adults who claim to have ADHD are pretending. The myth that

ADHD is just present in children is inaccurate because ADHD is a chronic condition that can persist into adulthood. In fact, research has shown that up to 70% of children with ADHD will continue to experience symptoms into adulthood which there are a number of reasons for: One reason is that the underlying neurobiology of ADHD is thought to be lifelong. Another reason is that the demands of adult life can be more challenging for people with ADHD. For example, adults with ADHD may have difficulty with tasks such as managing their time, staying organized, and meeting deadlines.

So, with that being said, let's not listen to the myths about ADHD, but rather focus on the facts. When we focus on the reality, it is much easier to accept and embrace our children who are neurodiverse. Now that we understand what ADHD is (and what it isn't), it's time to explore different strategies for parenting that will be beneficial for you and your child with ADHD.

Chapter 2:

Parenting Styles and Strategies

I'm not going to pretend like I'm the perfect parent. In fact, I sometimes feel like I'm doing everything wrong! However, the fact that I sometimes feel that way is proof that I am doing at least one thing right: I care enough to want to be better. When my son got diagnosed with ADHD, I knew that I wanted to help him as best as I could. I had no idea what that would look like, but I understood that my parenting style would need to change if I wanted to help my child effectively. In this chapter, I want to share with you different parenting styles and how to embrace empathy as part of your parenting style to better help your ADHDer. Every child is different, and every dynamic between a parent and a child is different, which is why there isn't a one-size-fits-all solution. However, there are certain techniques and tips that we can all embrace and adapt to fit our personal way of parenting.

In this chapter, we'll start by looking at how to see the world through your child's point of view. When we're able to see things from their perspective, we're more likely to be patient, kind, and empathetic in our parenting approach. We'll also look at how we can improve our child's self-esteem, even when they are facing difficulties due to their ADHD. We'll discover a couple of parenting techniques and how we can implement them into our daily lives, while continuing to connect with our children. We'll explore the importance of communication and active listening and how we can teach those skills to our ADHDers. We'll end this chapter by looking at how we can collaborate better with educators and professionals to help our children achieve their goals. So, with all of that waiting for us, let's jump straight into seeing the world through their eyes.

Seeing the World Through Their Eyes

A couple of years ago, I was watching my children play with their friends and I couldn't help but wonder what they were thinking. I noticed my little girl and her friends flapping their arms and drinking with their pinkies high in the air. Obviously, they were having a fairy tea party. As I moved my attention to the boys, I noticed that even though my son's two friends were sitting in the tree, playing pirate, my son was running around the tree, jumping and trying to snatch at them. In all honesty, it looked like they were playing two completely different games. Later that night as I put him to bed, I asked him if he had a good day and to my surprise, he smiled and said that it was *awesome*. In fact, he told me that when they were playing pirates, he felt the need to move his legs more than what the "ship" allowed him to, so he became the sea monster that the pirates were hunting. "Didn't you feel left out when you couldn't be a pirate anymore?" I asked him, expecting him to admit feeling disappointed. "No," he said with clarity, "Josh and Daniel needed some bonding time anyway since they had a fight earlier this week." I was in complete awe of my son's ability to problem-solve. Not only did he find a way to manage his energy and restless legs, but he was able to look past just playing and help his two friends join forces again.

As I walked from his room, I felt a sense of pride. I never thought I'd see the day where my ADHD son would be able to manage his life so well. I thought back to all the tears we had experienced in the past, all the breakdowns and the fights, and I couldn't help but smile. So, dear parent, if you're currently in a screaming or breakdown phase, I want to encourage you by saying that there is hope and the best way to discover that hope is by understanding their perspective, fostering a strong connection with your child, and nurturing their self-esteem.

Understanding Their Perspective

Children with ADHD experience the world differently than their neurotypical peers. To fully understand your child's perspective, you need to try and put yourself in their shoes. As they get older and learn the appropriate communication skills, they'll be able to explain their point of view to you more effectively, but until then, you'll need to understand their perspective without much of their input. There are three things that you need to keep in mind when you're trying to understand their perspective of the world:

- **Embrace Empathy:** When it's been a long week and everything seem to go wrong, it can be really hard to deal with ADHD-related issues while being empathetic. That doesn't make you a bad parent; it simply makes you human. You can remind yourself to be empathetic by putting yourself in their shoes. If you're also neurodivergent, it might be easier for you to do this. However, if you're not, imagine what it would be like to have ADHD. Look at the things your child had to face this week from their perspective. What were the challenges they had to deal with? By putting yourself in their shoes, you are much more likely to be empathetic toward them and not get frustrated.

- **Acknowledge Frustrations:** Another way that you can understand their perspective is by acknowledging the things that they might be frustrated about. Be empathic with their special frustrations, even when it's not something that would frustrate a neurotypical child. The best way for your child to open up to you is by letting them know that you understand their frustrations. For example, acknowledge that having to share with siblings might be a really difficult and frustrating thing, even though sharing is good.

- **Validate Their Struggles:** Understanding their perspective also requires you to validate their struggles. It's important for your ADHD child to feel understood. Often after an emotional situation or a frustration, children with ADHD can feel sensitive and scared that they might have overreacted, probably because many people will tell them that they did. As a parent, it's your job to help your child learn how to deal with their emotions and struggles, but it's also your job to help them feel understood and heard. Even when you don't agree with them, try your best to understand how they are feeling and express that to them with empathy.

Fostering a Strong Connection

Seeing the world through their eyes is helpful to understand their perspective better, but it can also be helpful in creating a strong connection between you and your child. Fostering a strong connection between parent and child can be tricky, even if your child is neurotypical. However, a strong parent-child connection is essential for a child's development. Children who have strong bonds with their parents are more likely to have high self-esteem and successful relationships with others. The best way to foster a strong connection is by spending quality time together.

Quality time doesn't mean that you have to spend hours and hours every day talking or playing with your child, but it does mean that you have to make time for activities that you both can enjoy together. By understanding their perspective, you'll start to have a better idea of what they might consider quality time. Your child with ADHD might not want to spend long periods of time building a puzzle, but they might be interested in going to the zoo with you and talking about all the different animals. The most important aspect of quality time is that you put away all distractions and focus on being present. When you spend quality time together, it will lead to trust and open communication.

Open communication and trust are two of the most essential keys to maintaining a strong connection. When your child feels like you can be trusted, they will be more likely to share with you openly. However, communication is a two-way street and therefore, you should also be prepared to share openly with your child. That might mean having difficult conversations from time to time, but it's essential that you don't try and hide things from them. For example, if a teacher reaches out to you with concern regarding your child, don't try to hide it from them. Instead, have an open conversation with them and ask them what they are struggling with. Allowing them to share their perspective will create a bond of trust and connection, which will show them that you love them unconditionally.

All children need unconditional love, whether they have ADHD or not. As parents, we often forget to express unconditional love in a way that children understand. We get busy and we assume that they know just how much we love them. Unfortunately, many children grow up not knowing that their parents love them unconditionally. You can express unconditional love to your child by

- **Telling Them That You Love Them Often:** Don't just assume that they know you love them. Say it out loud, every day.

- **Listening to Them:** When they talk to you, give them your full attention. Make eye contact, nod your head, and ask follow-up questions. Let them know that you're interested in what they have to say.

- **Being Supportive and Encouraging:** Let your child know that you believe in them and that you're there for them, no matter what. Encourage them to pursue their interests and to try new things.

- **Being Affectionate:** Show your child that you love them through physical touch, such as hugs, kisses, and cuddles. You can also express your love through words and actions.

- **Being Forgiving:** Everyone makes mistakes. When your child makes a mistake, don't hold it against them. Forgive them and move on.

Nurturing Self-Esteem and Resilience

When you see the world through your child's eyes, you'll be able to help them identify obstacles, along with strategies to deal with possible issues. In other words, you'll be able to help them build resilience while nurturing high self-esteem.

There are three specific ways that you can nurture a healthy self-esteem and build resilience in your ADHDer:

- **Celebrating Achievements:** Children with ADHD often struggle to stay on task, complete assignments, and meet expectations. This can lead to feelings of frustration, discouragement, and low self-esteem. Celebrating achievements, no matter how small, can help children with ADHD to build confidence and self-esteem. It can also help them to develop a sense of accomplishment and motivation. When children know that their hard work and effort is appreciated, they are more likely to continue to persevere in the face of challenges.

- **Teaching Coping Skills:** Teaching coping skills to your child with ADHD is important for a number of reasons. First, it can help them to manage their symptoms more effectively. Coping skills can help them to focus better, stay calm, and make better choices. Second, coping skills can help children with ADHD to succeed in school and in their personal lives, since coping skills can help them to stay on track and to manage their time more effectively. Finally, teaching coping skills to your child with ADHD can help them to develop resilience. Children with ADHD often face challenges in their lives, but coping skills can help them to cope with these challenges in a healthy way.

- **Encouraging Growth:** Encouraging growth can help your child to develop their full potential, since children with ADHD often have strengths and talents that can be nurtured and developed with the right support. Encouraging growth can also help them to overcome the challenges associated with ADHD, such as attention and self-control. With the right support, your ADHDer can learn to manage their challenges and succeed in school, at home, and in their relationships, while wanting to continue to grow and be better. Encouraging growth in your child with ADHD takes time and effort, but it's worth it. When you help your child to grow and develop, you're setting them up for success in life.

Positive Parenting Techniques

Positive parenting is a parenting approach that focuses on building a strong relationship with your child and teaching them through positive reinforcement and discipline. It is based on the belief that children learn best when they feel loved, supported, and respected. Positive parenting is especially important for children with ADHD, since positive parenting can reduce conflict and teach children with ADHD certain skills that they need in life. Positive parenting provides many benefits, such as improved behavior, increased self-esteem, and stronger parent-child relationships. Positive parenting is a journey, not a destination. It takes time and effort to learn and implement positive parenting strategies. But it is worth it for the benefits that it can provide for your child and your relationship with them. There are three elements of positive parenting that I would like to introduce to you: clear and consistent boundaries, positive reinforcement, and effective discipline.

Clear and Consistent Boundaries

The first element of positive parenting is setting and maintaining clear and consistent boundaries. Since children with ADHD often have difficulty with attention, organization, and self-control, it can lead to children who act out and experience behavioral challenges. When you have clear and consistent boundaries, it will help not only you as the parent, but also your child to understand what is appropriate and what is not. Boundaries will help your child understand that not everything they do is wrong, but that there are parameters that they need to act within. Clear and consistent boundaries help children with ADHD to understand what is expected of them and what the consequences will be if they don't meet those expectations. This helps them to feel safe and secure and to learn how to manage their behavior.

Here are three tips that you can use in order to set and maintain clear boundaries with your ADHD child:

- **Establish Rules:** Be clear and specific about the rules that you have with them. When setting boundaries, be clear and specific about what you expect of your child. For example, instead of saying "behave," say "please keep your hands and feet to yourself."

- **Be Consistent:** Once you have set boundaries, be consistent in enforcing them. This means following through with consequences, even when it is difficult. As soon as you're not consistent with boundaries, your child will notice and begin to take advantage of it. They might also get confused and it can lead to a lack of self-confidence, confused as to when something is inappropriate and when it's not. Along with consistency comes fair consequences, which we'll look at in the effective discipline section.

- **Use Positive Language:** Positive language is important when setting up clear and consistent boundaries with your ADHD child because it helps to create a positive and supportive environment. Positive language is also easier to understand and follow, since they'll have a clear picture of what's expected of them. Positive language also encourages responsibility because when you use positive language, you are not blaming or shaming your child; instead, you are helping them to see that their choices have consequences. Here are a couple of examples of positive language.

"I can see that you're excited, but please walk inside."

"I know that you're busy playing, but it's time to clean up your toys so that we can spend time together as a family."

"You can choose between doing your homework now or after dinner."

"I'm proud of you for trying your best. Let's try again tomorrow."

It is also important to remember that boundaries are not meant to be punishing. They are meant to help children with ADHD to learn and grow. When setting and enforcing boundaries, be sure to do so in a loving and supportive way.

Positive Reinforcement and Rewards

One of my favorite techniques of positive parenting is implementing a rewards system. I can honestly say that this system changed the game not only in my child with ADHD, but also my other children. In short, positive reinforcement involves rewarding children for their good behavior. This can be done through praise, stickers, small gifts, or other privileges. Rewards can also be used to help children learn new skills or to break bad habits. There are so many benefits to positive reinforcement, one of which is that it can help your child with their behavior. When children are rewarded for their good behavior, they are more likely to repeat that behavior in the future. Positive reinforcement can also help to boost children's self-esteem. When children feel good about themselves, they are more likely to be motivated to succeed. However, when implementing a positive reward system, there are a few things you need to keep in mind:

- **Praise and Encouragement:** The first reward most children seek is approval from their parents, so be sure to give verbal praise and encouragement when they are performing a task well. However, you shouldn't use praise as a bargaining chip like you might use other rewards. For example, don't say, "I'll tell you you're smart once you finish your homework." Rather try, "You are so smart and I can see that you're trying really hard. Let's continue to work on homework for another 10 minutes and then we can go get ice cream."

- **Be Specific and Timely:** Since ADHD children struggle to remain focused on one task, it's important to be specific about what behavior you're praising or rewarding. For example, instead of saying "Good job," try saying "Good job sitting still and paying attention during story time." If you're not specific and timely, it might cause confusion as to what they're being praised for.

- **Variety of Rewards:** Children with ADHD can get bored easily, so use a variety of rewards to keep them motivated. Rewards can be tangible, such as stickers or toys, or it can be intangible, such as special attention or allowing them to do their favorite activity over the weekend.

- **Offer Choices:** Children with ADHD often feel like they don't have control over their lives. Offering them choices can help them feel more in control and make them more likely to cooperate. That way you'll also ensure that they're getting a reward that they want.

Effective Discipline

The final element of positive parenting that I want to discuss is effective discipline. As a parent of an ADHDer, you probably already know that discipline can be tricky. When it comes to disciplining your child, there is a balance that needs to be managed between having boundaries versus running your home like it's the military. It's important for all children to feel a sense of safety at home, knowing that even if they make a mistake, they will be loved. However, they also need discipline in order to grow into well-functioning adults. Effective discipline is an important element of positive parenting with an ADHD child. It can help children learn to manage their behavior and develop the skills they need to be successful in life. There are three methods of discipline that are highly effective on most ADHD children:

- **Natural Consequences:** Natural consequences are the logical outcomes of a child's behavior. They are often the most effective way to discipline children with ADHD, because they help children learn to take responsibility for their actions and make better choices. It is important to choose natural consequences that are directly related to the child's behavior and that are age-appropriate. For natural consequences to be effective, you first need to explain the consequence to your child ahead of time. Then, once the consequence happens, talk them through it and help them to manage it effectively so that they can learn in the future.

- **Time-Outs and Cool-Offs:** Time-outs and cool-offs are effective discipline methods for ADHD kids because they give them a chance to calm down and regain control of their emotions. They can also help children learn to take responsibility for their behavior. Time-outs involve removing a child from a situation for a short period of time, usually 1-5 minutes. The goal of a time-out is to give the child a chance to calm down and rethink their behavior. Cool-offs are similar to time-outs, but they allow the child to stay in the same room or area as you. The goal of a cool-off is to give the child a chance to calm down and regain control of their emotions without removing them from the situation.

- **Consistency:** Children with ADHD need to know what is expected of them in order to be successful. Make sure your rules are clear and easy to understand. Be consistent in enforcing the rules, even when it's difficult. If something is against the rules today, make sure that it's also against the rules tomorrow.

Remember, the goal of discipline is not to punish your child, but to teach them how to behave appropriately. By using these methods of discipline effectively, you can help your ADHD child learn and grow. Positive parenting doesn't begin and end at home, though. You have to also make use of positive parenting methods at school and other social engagements, which is why we need to learn how to collaborate with educators and professionals.

Collaborating With Educators and Professionals

As a parent of a child with ADHD, the mama-bear in me is often overly protective. I'll do anything to protect my children from any harm. Yet, I've noticed over the years that I can sometimes be a little...

sensitive, especially when it comes to my child with ADHD. I realized this after a parent-teacher conference. First, I spoke to my daughter's teacher. I nodded and listened as she told me that my daughter was doing great and that she enjoyed speaking to her friends a lot. The teacher told me that my daughter was very creative and often made up stories, prompting the rest of her friends to play along. However, she also mentioned that we might need to pay a little bit of extra attention on math homework since she was slightly behind the rest of her friends. I nodded, agreed to help with the math, and left feeling like my child was getting great care.

After speaking to my daughter's teacher, it was time to speak to my ADHD son's teacher. She shared that he was trying really hard, but that he often disrupted the class with his stories, although he would always apologize afterward. She shared how he was doing really well in art and English, but that we might want to focus a little bit on science at home. Immediately, I felt attacked and jumped into defense mode. I explained that he had ADHD and that disrupting the class was due to that. I also said that not being good at science isn't the end of the world. The teacher looked at me, patiently waited for me to finish my rant, and said, "I know, Mrs. Michaels. I was actually complimenting his manners and his emotional intelligence for apologizing after every incident. I'm also not saying that he should become a scientist, but it's my job as a teacher to help my students in the areas where they need it, which in his case, is in the science department." She then showed me a very creative, at-home science set which she would recommend we invest in, since the practical element would help my son grasp the theoretical concepts. I walked out of there feeling miserable as I realized that I didn't have to fight the teachers all the time, but rather work together.

Unfortunately, many parents with neurodivergent children are very protective due to educators and other professionals being unempathetic toward ADHD children based on the myths we discussed in Chapter 1. And even though some teachers don't get it and don't seem to want the best for your child, not all teachers are like that. It's a hard pill to swallow, I know, but it's essential that you stop fighting everything teachers and professionals say, and instead find teachers and professionals that you trust and with whom you can collaborate. It all starts by learning how to navigate the school system.

Navigating the School System

Navigating the school system when you have a child with ADHD can be challenging. However, it is important to do so in order to ensure that your child receives the support and services they need to succeed. But what does it even mean to navigate the school system? Well, it has a double meaning. On the one hand, it means understanding how the school system works in order for you to be prepared and stay involved in your child's education. On the other hand, it means helping your child understand what they're getting into and what protocols to follow. The first step to navigating the school system is understanding and making use of the Individualized Education Program (IEP) process.

The Individualized Education Program

The IEP is a plan developed to ensure that children with identified disabilities receive specialized instructions (University of Washington, 2019). An IEP is also a legal document that outlines the special education and related services that a student with a disability needs to succeed in school and they are required by the Individuals With Disabilities Education Act (IDEA), a federal law that ensures that all students with disabilities have access to appropriate public education. To qualify for an IEP, a student must have a disability that meets the criteria outlined, and ADHD is one of the disabilities that qualifies for an IEP.

The IEP is developed by a team of educators and professionals, including the student's parents or guardians, which means that you get to be involved! The team meets to review the student's evaluation data and develop goals and objectives for the student, and also develops a plan for providing the student with the accommodations and modifications they need to succeed in school. IEPs are reviewed and updated at least once a year, or more often if needed. This ensures that the IEP is meeting the student's needs and that the student is making progress toward their goals. If you have a child with ADHD, it is important to understand the IEP process and how to use an IEP to help your child succeed in school. So, be sure to attend IEP meetings and communicate with educators often and openly. You might just find that there are teachers who want your child to succeed just as much as you do, who will help them in any way that they can.

After my meeting with my son's teacher, I took a hard look in the mirror and decided to assume that his teacher wanted what was best for my child and that they were not out to make life more difficult for him. The teacher was even kind enough to create a system with me where I was able to let her know ahead of time if my son was having a bad day or feeling more emotional than usual. In return, she would keep me updated and help me to work in peace, knowing that he was taken care of. Speaking to the teacher openly made me realize just how important it is to advocate for your child's needs.

Advocating for Your Child's Needs

Advocating for your child doesn't mean causing chaos and havoc whenever something happens that you don't agree with. It often means listening to others and then communicating your child's needs in a way that is respectful, yet firm. Here are several tips on how to effectively advocate for your child's needs at school:

- **Be Prepared:** Before you meet with your child's teacher or other school staff, take some time to prepare. This will help you to be clear and concise in your communication. Know what you want to talk about and what questions you want to ask.

- **Be Specific:** When talking to school staff about your child's ADHD, be specific about the symptoms that your child experiences and how they impact their learning and behavior. Don't try to sugarcoat things and be specific as to what you're expecting from the school in return.

- **Be Positive:** Focus on the things that you want the school to do to support your child, rather than the things that you don't want them to do. Being positive will set the atmosphere for the staff and it will show them that you're not out to catch them doing something wrong.

- **Be Collaborative:** Work with the school staff to develop a plan that meets your child's needs and helps them to succeed. Listen to what they have to say and trust that they sometimes know best.

- **Be Persistent:** Don't be afraid to follow up with school staff to ensure that your child is receiving the support that they need. You can be persistent and respectful at the same time; it just takes a little bit of patience.

Other tips that will also help you to advocate for your child's needs more clearly is when you know the staff at school and build rapport with them. This will make communication much easier for all parties involved. It's also helpful to communicate with other parents of ADHDers to see whether you're all on the same page and whether you might notice the same need. Finally, learn about your child's rights and make sure that you understand them. This will give you a guideline as to what is okay and what isn't. Collaborating doesn't stop at school, though. You also need to be able to collaborate with therapists and specialists.

Collaborating With Therapists and Specialists

Collaborating with therapists and specialists is essential when your child has ADHD, since therapists and specialists can provide your child with the support and services they need to manage their ADHD symptoms and thrive. There are three major reasons why it's beneficial to collaborate with therapists and specialists in order to get the best for your child:

- **Assessment and Diagnosis:** Therapists and specialists can assess your child to determine if they have ADHD and other co-occurring conditions. They can also help you understand your child's unique strengths and weaknesses.

- **Treatment and Support:** Therapists and specialists can provide your child with a variety of treatments and support services, including individual therapy, group therapy, and family counseling. They can also help you develop a behavior plan to manage your child's behavior at home and in school.

- **Education and Training:** Therapists and specialists can educate you and your child about ADHD and its management. They can also provide training to your child's teachers and other school staff on how to support your child in the classroom.

It's important that you find therapists and specialists that you trust. When you don't trust the professionals you're working with, it can cause some confusion for your child, since they will most likely pick up on your hesitation. Here are some tips for collaborating with therapists and specialists:

- **Be Transparent:** It's essential that you are open and honest with your child's therapists and specialists. The more information they have about your child, the better equipped they will be to help.

- **Listen:** You have to be willing to listen to the suggestions of your child's therapists and specialists. They have expertise in ADHD and can provide valuable guidance.

- **Be Proactive:** One of the best ways to collaborate with specialists is by being proactive in communicating with them. Don't wait until there is a problem to reach out.

- **Be Involved:** It's essential that you're involved in your child's treatment. Attend therapy sessions and participate in family counseling. This will help you to stay informed of your child's progress and to support them at home.

Collaborating with therapists and specialists can make a big difference in the life of a child with ADHD. By working together, you can create a supportive environment for your child to learn and grow. By embracing positive parenting, you'll make a massive difference in the life of your child, which is what we're all hoping to achieve, after all. In the next chapter, we'll look at the next step of helping your child with ADHD, which is to establish effective routines.

Chapter 3:

Establishing Effective Routines

You know in the movies when they overdramatize just how hectic mornings can be? Yes, those scenes where the lunch boxes are still empty by the time the kids need to leave for school, and the dog is throwing up on the carpet, and the children are fighting, and dad is looking for his keys, and mom is trying to get everyone to eat their breakfast, and, and, and... It's a madhouse, and I used to watch movies or TV series where this would happen all the time, laughing along with the chaos and at just how ridiculous it is. One day, as I was enjoying an episode of *Modern Family*, this exact scene was playing out. As I laughed, my son walked in, pointed at the screen and said, "That's like our home!" Before I could convince him that it wasn't the case, he left the room, on to his next mission, but it made me wonder about our mornings and how hectic things sometimes were.

As I returned my gaze to the show, I realized that my son was right. We were the crazy family with the chaotic morning routine! I didn't know whether I should laugh or cry as I realized the only consistent thing about our morning routines is the fact that something is always missing, whether it be keys, phones, remotes, or textbooks. It didn't bother me too much, until I remembered reading somewhere that having effective routines is essential for all kids, especially ones with ADHD. In typical mom behavior, I felt guilty and ashamed of the routines in our home or, more accurately, the lack of routines. You see, I realized that it wasn't just our morning routine that needed work, but all of them throughout the day! So, I made it my mission to establish effective routines to help my children (and myself) where I could.

Perhaps you've experienced the chaos of mornings yourself, or maybe your routines need some work in other areas. Regardless, in this chapter, we'll get to the bottom of things and find a way to improve and establish routines that actually work. We'll look at three different routines that every ADHDer needs: a morning routine, an after-school routine, and a bedtime routine. Let's start at the beginning and look at what an effective morning routine consists of.

Morning Routines

Morning routines are absolutely essential for children with ADHD, since they require structure in order to be on time, be prepared, and have everything they need. Creating a morning routine enables your ADHDer to take a moment to think about their day. The beauty of a morning routine is that you can put activities in the routine that you know will help your child with their daily functions. For example, part of our morning routine consists of the kids lining up at the front door and naming all the things in their backpack—lunchbox, permission slip, textbooks, gym shoes, etc. Whatever they need for the day, we run through a checklist to make sure that it's all there. This all forms part of the four key elements of a morning routine: wake-up time, a schedule, breakfast, and preparing for the day.

Consistent Wake-Up Times

By now we know and understand that children with ADHD have difficulty with executive functioning skills such as planning, organizing, and time management. A consistent wake-up time can help to provide a structure and routine that can help children with ADHD to manage their time more effectively and to be more successful in school and other activities. Here are some of the specific benefits of consistent wake-up times for children with ADHD:

- **Improved Sleep Quality:** Did you know that children with ADHD are more likely to have sleep problems than children without ADHD? Luckily, a consistent wake-up time can help to regulate the body's natural sleep-wake cycle, which can lead to better sleep quality. So, by helping them to get up in the morning, you are also helping them to get better rest during the night.

- **Reduced Morning Stress:** If you don't want your mornings to look like something from a sitcom, a morning routine is the way to go. When children have a consistent wake-up time, they know what to expect in the morning and can get ready for school at a leisurely pace. This can help to reduce morning stress and make it easier for children to start their day off on the right foot.

- **Improved Attention and Focus:** Children who get enough sleep are better able to pay attention and focus. A consistent wake-up time can help to ensure that children are getting the sleep they need to be successful in school and other activities. Since your ADHDer most likely struggles with staying focused, this is a good way to help them indirectly.

- **Improved Mood and Behavior:** Children who are well-rested are more likely to be in a good mood and to behave appropriately. A consistent wake-up time can help to improve children's overall well-being. No one wants to deal with a grumpy cat all day long, so by giving your child a good, calming morning routine, they'll be able to regulate their emotions much better.

If you have a child with ADHD, it is important to establish a consistent wake-up time and to stick to it as much as possible, even on weekends and during school breaks. This may take some time and effort, but it is worth it in the long run.

Visual Morning Schedule

A visual morning schedule is a tool that you can use to help your ADHD child understand what is expected of them every morning. It will allow them to see the routine they have to follow, which will also prevent them from stressing over forgetting something in their routine. A visual morning schedule can help your ADHD child to

- **Understand Expectations:** A visual schedule breaks down the morning routine into small, manageable steps, which can make it easier for them to follow.

- **Reduce Anxiety and Stress:** Children with ADHD often experience anxiety and stress when they are unsure of what to expect. A visual schedule can help them to feel more in control and reduce their anxiety levels.

- **Increase Independence:** A visual schedule can help children with ADHD learn to complete their morning routine on their own. This can boost their self-esteem and confidence.

- **Improve Time Management:** A visual schedule can help children with ADHD learn how to manage their time more effectively. This can be beneficial in all areas of their lives, including school, sports, and social activities.

Creating a visual morning schedule will require some time and effort from your side, but I highly recommend it! Here are some tips for creating a visual morning schedule for your child:

- Use pictures instead of words.

- Keep it clear and simple.

- Place the schedule in a prominent location.

- Make it interactive if possible (such as a whiteboard where they have to tick off everything they've done).

- Review the schedule with your child on a daily basis to make sure they understand the importance of every task.

If you are struggling to create a visual morning schedule for your child with ADHD, there are many resources available to help you. You can find pre-made visual schedules online or at specialty stores.

Breakfast and Nutrition

We've all heard the saying that breakfast is the most important meal of the day, right? Well, this is especially true when it comes to children with ADHD. Eating a nutritious breakfast can help your child control their ADHD symptoms and it will give them the energy that they need to succeed in school. Breakfast can help children with ADHD in many ways, such as the following:

- improved attention and focus

- reduced hyperactivity and impulsiveness

- improved behavior

- improved academic performance

In addition to these benefits, eating a healthy breakfast can also help to improve children's overall health and well-being. Children who eat breakfast are less likely to be overweight or obese, and they are also less likely to develop chronic diseases such as diabetes and heart disease later in life. With that being said, here are a couple of tips for choosing a healthy breakfast for your child:

- **High Protein:** Make sure to choose foods that are high in protein and complex carbohydrates. Protein helps to keep blood sugar levels stable, and complex carbohydrates take longer to digest than simple carbohydrates, which helps to keep children feeling full and energized for longer. Good sources of protein include eggs, yogurt, cheese, nuts, and seeds. Good sources of complex carbohydrates include whole grains, fruits, and vegetables.

- **Limit Sugar:** Sugary foods and drinks can cause blood sugar levels to spike and crash quickly, which can lead to hyperactivity and impulsiveness. Instead, offer children water, milk, or unsweetened juice. Be sure to read the labels on breakfast cereals, since they are often filled with sugar.

- **Have Fun:** You can make breakfast a fun and enjoyable experience by creating a relaxed and positive atmosphere at breakfast-time. Avoid rushing or nagging your child to eat. Instead, try to make breakfast a time for bonding and socializing.

Prepare in Advance

Preparing in advance is an important part of a morning routine for children with ADHD. It can help to reduce stress and anxiety, improve time management skills, reduce conflict, and boost confidence. By following these tips, you can help your child with ADHD start their day off on the right foot and have a successful day at school.

- **Prepare the Night Before:** As much as possible, prepare for the morning routine the night before. This could include packing lunches, setting out clothes, and making sure that all backpacks and supplies are ready to go.

- **Set Realistic Expectations:** Don't expect children with ADHD to get ready for school in the same amount of time as other children. Give them plenty of time to complete each task and be prepared to offer help and support if needed.

- **Take Breaks:** Children with ADHD often have difficulty staying focused for long periods of time. Schedule breaks into the morning routine so that children can take a moment to rest and recharge.

- **Make it Fun:** Children are more likely to follow a routine if it is fun and engaging. Try to make the morning routine as enjoyable as possible by playing music, dancing, or playing games.

All of this together creates the perfect morning routine for you and your entire family, not just the ADHDers. However, the morning is only the first part of the day. If we want our children to be healthy, happy, and thriving, we also need an after-school routine.

After-School Routine

A good after-school routine should include a mix of activities, such as homework, physical activity, and relaxation. It is important to choose activities that your child enjoys and that are appropriate for their age and developmental level. For example, a younger child with ADHD might benefit from a routine that includes a snack, some outdoor play, and then some quiet time to read or listen to music. An older child with ADHD might benefit from a routine that includes a snack, some time to work on homework, and then some time to participate in an extracurricular activity that they enjoy. It is also important to be flexible with your child's after-school routine. There will be days when they need more time to work on homework or when they just need to relax. Be willing to adjust the routine as needed, but try to stick to it as much as possible. A good after-school routine consists of five elements, which we'll look at now.

Unwind Time

Having unwind time is essential for your child after a long day at school. Your ADHDer is most likely mentally exhausted after school, filled with pent-up energy and perhaps even frustrations. Allowing them some time to de-stress in whatever way they prefer will help them to manage their energy and get rid of the overstimulated feeling that many ADHD kids feel after school. Unwind time also helps your child to regulate their emotions in a healthy way. It will give them the opportunity to express and deal with the emotions that they might have been avoiding all day, like anger, frustration, or excitement. During unwind time they also have the opportunity to reduce impulsive behavior. They'll start to learn that during unwind time they'll be free to do what they want, so they'll reduce their impulsive behavior throughout the rest of the day. However, it's also important that ADHDers learn that not everything is okay during unwind time, since certain activities can make them even more frustrated or overstimulated.

Here's some tips on how to create an unwind time for your child with ADHD:

- Choose activities that are calming and relaxing, such as reading, listening to music, or playing with calming toys.

- Avoid activities that might lead to overstimulation or too much excitement, such as watching television or immediately doing homework.

- Set a specific time for unwinding and stick to it as much as possible. This will help them to experience structure within the unwinding.

- Create a quiet space that is comfortable for unwinding, such as a special nook in the living room or a playroom.

- Allow your child to choose between activities during unwind time so that they'll feel motivated and actually participate.

Homework Organization

After unwind time, they'll have time for homework. To help your child with homework, it's essential that you have a designated area with all the supplies ready and organized. By having an organized space, you'll help them to have a calmer mind regarding homework and it will help them to remain focused when they don't have to run around trying to find whatever they need to do their work. One of the best ways that I've learned to help my son with ADHD do his homework is by creating a visual homework schedule. We'll sit together and go through all his subjects, checking to see if he has any homework in each one. Then we'll write the assignments on a small whiteboard, along with the dates when it has to be finished. If it's a big task that is due soon, we also create a progress bar that he can color in as he makes progress. Creating a schedule for the homework will help your child to stay on track, as it also serves as a reminder.

If your child gets easily overwhelmed or you notice that their attention span is really limited after a long day of sitting still and doing homework, you can break their homework into manageable chunks. Offer them short breaks in-between different assignments or questions that they've finished. For example, do five math problems, then allow a ten-minute break. However, if your child is hyperfocused, don't offer the break, since that might destroy their focus altogether.

Physical Activity

Every after-school routine needs some physical activity, especially if your child has ADHD. This can be in the form of a sports club or a team that they might be part of, or it can include playing outside and riding their bike. Physical exercise can help release pent-up energy, which will improve their focus. Many ADHDers find it easier to be physically active before attempting homework, since it gives them an outlet for their energy and will help them to refocus. Structured activities such as a team sport are particularly beneficial for children with ADHD, since it provides them with rules to stick to, but also allows physical freedom. In addition to these benefits, physical activity is also important for overall health and well-being. It can help to strengthen bones and muscles, reduce the risk of obesity and chronic diseases, and promote better sleep.

Managing Screen Time

While it can be tempting to give in to screen time the whole day, it's essential that you help your child to not spend all his or her time on a screen of some sorts. You have to set clear rules for screen time to ensure that it doesn't interfere with their homework and physical activities, or with their family time. Time blindness often occurs when screens are involved, which means that your ADHDer might completely lose track of time as they watch a story, and before they know it, they've missed their homework schedule. One way to solve this is by setting a timer, or limiting the screen time completely to one hour a day. This will promote time management and it will also help with their overall health. It's absolutely crucial to balance screen time if you want to maintain a well-rounded routine for your child.

Family Time

The final element of an after-school routine is family time. Be sure to set aside time every day that is dedicated family time. During this time, you and your family can engage in activities together, preferably not screen-related activities. For example, playing board games or building a jigsaw puzzle together as a family can be a great way to end the day together. You can also play outside or go for a bike ride as a family if that is more your thing. You should use family time to bond and connect with your child, providing emotional support while fostering stronger bonds amongst everyone in the family. Positive family interactions will help your child to have better emotional well-being and it will also help navigate the relationship between ADHD children and non-ADHD children.

As the after-school routine comes to an end, it's time to focus on the bedtime routine, which most definitely shouldn't be overlooked or rushed.

Bedtime Routine

Children with ADHD often have difficulty winding down at night, so a bedtime routine is vital, since it can help them to signal to their bodies and minds that it is time to prepare for sleep. There are many benefits to having a bedtime routine, such as the fact that it promotes healthy sleep habits and it can improve their emotional stability. However, in this section, I want to focus on answering what makes a good bedtime routine. There are three elements to a bedtime routine, so let's have a closer look at each.

Consistent Bedtime

The first element of importance for a successful bedtime routine is consistency. Not only is it essential to be consistent with the routine every night, but to also be consistent with the bedtime. A consistent bedtime can help your child with ADHD to

- regulate the body's natural sleep-wake cycle, also known as the circadian rhythm.

- provide structure and predictability in which they can thrive.

- provide the body with enough time to calm down and rest before the next day.

In addition to the benefits listed above, a consistent bedtime can also help to improve a child's mood, behavior, and overall well-being. When children are well-rested, they are better able to focus, learn, and regulate their emotions. If you're not sure how to create a consistent bedtime, here are a couple of things to keep in mind:

- Choose a bedtime based on your child's needs.

- Stick to the same bedtime, even over holidays and weekends.

- Create a relaxing atmosphere by removing all distractions.

- Avoid screentime at least one hour before bed.

- Be consistent with enforcing the bedtime routine.

Bedtime Activities

Calming bedtime activities can help your child to get into the mood for sleeping. Helping them to unwind by implementing various bedtime activities can improve their rest and their mood significantly. They will also be less defiant when they hear that it's time for bed if they've been preparing. Calming bedtime activities include taking a warm bath, reading a book, or talking with their siblings about their day. Activities to avoid before bed include screen time and other activities that might hype them up. As the parent, you can create a relaxing bedtime environment by dimming the lights and making sure that their bedding is comfortable. Make sure to start the bedtime activities early enough so that they'll be calm by the time they have to sleep.

Part of bedtime activities should include avoiding sugary drinks and caffeinated foods. Instead, opt for a healthy snack that will boost their melatonin levels, the hormone that helps you to feel sleepy. Bananas are a great source of melatonin, as well as cherries, pineapples, oranges, oats, rice, barley, and almonds.

Mindfulness and Relaxation

The final element of a good bedtime routine is mindfulness and relaxation. Mindfulness practices can help your child for several reasons, including

- **Reduced Anxiety:** Children with ADHD often have high levels of stress and anxiety, which can make it difficult to fall asleep and stay asleep. Mindfulness and relaxation techniques can help to calm the mind and body, making it easier to wind down for bed.

- **Improved Focus:** Mindfulness and relaxation techniques can help train the mind to focus on the present moment, which can be helpful for both falling asleep and staying asleep.

- **Quality Sleep:** When children are relaxed and focused, they are more likely to have a good night's sleep. Mindfulness and relaxation techniques can help to improve sleep quality by reducing stress, anxiety, and hyperactivity.

Here are a couple of mindfulness and relaxation methods that you can try before bed to help your child relax and rest (Simram, 2022):

- **Deep breathing:** Deep breathing is a simple and effective way to relax the mind and body. To do deep breathing, have your child sit or lie down in a comfortable position. Place one hand on their chest and the other hand on their stomach. Have them inhale slowly and deeply through their nose, allowing their stomach to rise. Then, have them exhale slowly through their mouth, allowing their stomach to fall. Repeat this for several minutes.

- **Progressive muscle relaxation:** Progressive muscle relaxation is a technique that involves tensing and relaxing different muscle groups in the body. To do progressive muscle relaxation, have your child start by tensing the muscles in their feet. Hold the tension for a few seconds, then relax the muscles. Repeat this with each muscle group in the body, working your way up from the feet to the head.

- **Guided imagery:** Guided imagery is a technique that involves using visualization to relax the mind and body. To do guided imagery, have your child close their eyes and imagine a relaxing scene. For example, they could imagine a beach, a forest, or a meadow. Have them focus on the details of the scene, such as the sights, sounds, smells, and feelings.

With these effective routines, your child will feel safe, motivated, and free to live without fear of doing something wrong or forgetting something important. Remember that routines might not be successful overnight. Keep going, even when your child seems to not react positively at first. Give it at least two weeks before making a call on whether it's working for your family or not. Now that we've covered the importance of keeping a consistent schedule, we should also look at how to effectively communicate with our children, as well as helping them to communicate effectively with others. More of that in the next chapter!

Chapter 4:

Cultivating Effective

Communication

Having clear and effective communication between you and your child can sometimes feel impossible. While you say one thing, they perceive another, and vice versa! This leads to endless miscommunications, and it can even lead to frustration and anger. So, what can we do about it? Well, as the parent, we need to learn how to cultivate effective communication with your child. Effective communication is built on listening and validating your child's emotions and experiences, establishing and expressing clear expectations, and building trust and resilience. By fostering open dialogue, trust, and resilience, you'll be able to create a supportive environment that empowers your child to thrive, despite the challenges of ADHD. In Chapter One, we touched on some of these topics briefly, but in this chapter, we'll dive into it more deeply. This comprehensive approach will promote understanding, collaboration, and emotional well-being within the family. However, before we jump into the theory, I want to share with you a personal story about communication.

I'm not proud to admit it, as most parents probably wouldn't be, but I sometimes get frustrated with my children. It often feels as if I'm talking to a wall where I get zero response. Most of the times, I am a pretty patient person and I pride myself in my ability to remain calm and not get annoyed when I have to repeat the same sentence three times. However, sometimes we have bad days, as most people do. I wish as a parent of a neurodivergent child that bad days would automatically skip you or take pity on you, but unfortunately, that's not the case. Before I implemented better ADHD management rules and skills into our daily lives, I often felt completely alone with all the struggles. I would repeat and repeat and repeat every question, every sentence, and every request for my son, and felt absolutely guilty whenever I got frustrated by his lack of understanding or his forgetfulness.

If you've ever felt guilty for being frustrated or even annoyed at your neurodivergent child, let me take the load off your shoulders and tell you that you're not alone and that it doesn't mean that you're a bad parent. Even more, I want to encourage you with some hope—it doesn't have to be this way! There are many ways that we as the parents can improve our own communication and with the same breath, help our children. Since communication really is the key to all relationships, it's essential that we find new ways to communicate so that both parties can understand the task at hand. Learning these techniques will allow you and your child the ability to communicate to one another without worrying about misunderstandings. It will be as if the two of you have your own secret language and I promise you, it will be amazing. Let's start by exploring the importance of active listening and validating their emotions. However, don't assume that all of this will magically happen and be perfect within a week. Learning how to communicate with your child might take some time, so be kind to yourself and to your child.

Active Listening and Validations

Active listening is more than just nodding your head in agreement. Physically, it might look like that's all there is to it, but when you practice active listening with your ADHD child, you are actually giving them a much larger gift: validation. Most children, especially children who are neurodivergent, are often confused with their own feelings and all they want is to hear that they make sense. They want to know that it's okay to get excited about the small things and memorize all the names of the ducks at the pond. They also want to know that it's okay to be mad at their friends or even embarrassed by certain behavior. When you listen actively to your children, you are giving them a safe space to acknowledge their true feelings. In other words, active listening is a communication skill that involves paying attention to what someone is saying, understanding what they mean, and responding in a way that shows you understand. It's not just hearing the words they say, but also trying to understand their feelings, their perspective, and what they're trying to communicate.

The Power of Listening

Active listening doesn't come naturally to everyone. In many cases, we need to work on it to ensure that we listen in a way that is validating the other person's emotions. As a parent, there are three parts of active listening that you need to focus on:

- **Being Mindful:** I know it might sound strange to think that you need to be mindful when you're listening to your child, but trust me, this is a gamechanger. Being mindful when you're listening means that you are totally aware of your surroundings and the context of the conversation. In other words, you're able to put yourself in their shoes. You can showcase mindfulness by asking open-ended questions, allowing your child to express what they're feeling even more (Fletcher, 2022). You can also be mindful of your body language and the nonverbal signs your child is signaling to you.

- **Reflective Responses:** When you're listening actively, you need to reflect back what you heard to show that you've been listening and that you understand what they're saying. This can be done by paraphrasing what they've said, or by asking clarifying questions. You can also reflect by summing up what you think your child is thinking or feeling, allowing them the opportunity to either agree or disagree with you (CDC, 2023).

- **Avoiding Judgment:** As you listen to your child, no matter how strange their stories might be or how much you disagree with what they're saying, it's important that you don't show any judgment. By showing judgment, you'll subconsciously send the message that you don't understand them and that they are weird. Chances are that they'll retract from you and be reluctant to engage in open dialogue with you again. Keep your judgments to yourself, and rather focus on the picture from their point of view.

Validating Emotions and Experiences

Part of active listening is validating your child's emotions and experiences. It's essential that you refrain from dismissing their emotions or how they've experienced a certain event. Even when you didn't perceive it the same way that they did, your job is to first listen. Later, when you give advice, you can help them to see things from the other side of the coin, but while you're listening, it's essential that you don't dismiss their feelings. Validating emotions and experiences is an important part of active listening, especially with children who have ADHD. It shows your child that you understand and accept them, even when they are feeling or behaving in a way that you don't agree with.

One of the best ways to validate emotions and experiences in your child is by being empathetic. We spoke about being empathetic in Chapter 2, so if you need a quick reminder, feel free to jump back in time and have a quick recap. It is important to note that validating your child's emotions does not mean that you have to agree with their behavior. For example, if your child is throwing a tantrum, you can validate their emotions by saying, "I can see that you're feeling angry right now." However, you should also set clear expectations for behavior and let your child know that there are consequences for bad behavior while being empathetic to the situation.

Validating your child's emotions and experiences is an important part of active listening and parenting. It helps your child to feel understood and accepted, which can lead to a stronger relationship between you and your child. By validating their emotions, you are creating a safe space for them to express themselves freely.

Encouraging Open Dialogue

The final element of active listening and validation that you need to encourage is having open dialogue with your child. Open dialogue doesn't mean that they get to speak to you however they want to, but it does mean that you are a safe space for them to come with questions and concerns. Even when questions seem scary or awkward, make sure that you embrace open dialogue and answer the questions as best as you can. If you're busy with something else and can't give the conversation your full attention, you should either pause what you're doing or set aside a specific time when you and your child can chat about the topic they had in mind. If you want your child to have open dialogue with you, it's important that they also witness open dialogue. You have to model the positive communication that you want to see in your child, so be open with what you're feeling and ask questions when you're wondering about something.

Setting Clear Expectations

Other than active listening, effective communication also requires clear expectations. We spoke about setting boundaries during Chapter 2, and in many ways, expectations and boundaries go hand-in-hand. Since children with ADHD often have difficulty with impulse control and organization, it can be helpful to provide them with clear and concise instructions and know exactly what is expected from them. Setting clear expectations requires you to be consistent. It is important to be consistent with your expectations and consequences because this will help your child to know what to expect and will make it easier for them to follow the rules. When you're not consistent, neither will their behavior be consistent. Here are some tips for setting clear expectations with your child who has ADHD:

- **Be Specific.** Don't just say, "Clean your room." Instead, say, "Put your toys away in the toy box, make your bed, and put your dirty clothes in the hamper."

- **Break it Down:** By breaking tasks down into smaller steps, you will make the task less daunting for your child and help them to stay on track. For example, instead of saying, "Write your essay," break it down into smaller steps, such as "Choose a topic," "Brainstorm ideas," "Write an outline," "Write the first draft," and "Edit the final draft."

- **Provide Visual Cues.** Children with ADHD often learn best visually, so try to use visual cues to help them understand your expectations. For example, you could create a checklist of chores that your child needs to complete, or use a timer to show them how long they have to complete a task.

Setting clear expectations is an important part of effective communication with your child who has ADHD. By following the tips above, you can help your child to understand and follow your expectations. This will lead to a more harmonious and productive relationship between you and your child.

Building Trust and Resilience

Effective communication also requires building trust and resilience which are essential for effective communication between you and your ADHD child. When your child trusts you, they are more likely to open up to you and share their thoughts and feelings. Resilience is the ability to bounce back from setbacks and challenges. When your child is resilient, they are more likely to persevere in the face of difficulty. Building trust and resilience might be challenging and it won't happen overnight, but it will help you and your child to communicate clearly and learn to trust one another. There are three elements to consider when it comes to building trust and resilience as part of effective communication skills: the building of the trust, having problem-solving skills up your sleeve, and being resilient and having coping strategies to deal with life's chaos.

Building Trusting Relationships

Building trust needs to be a priority for you and your child. One of the best ways to build trust with your ADHDer is by keeping promises. No matter how big or small the promise is that you make, you have to stick to it if you want your child to trust you regardless of everything else that might be happening in the world. Think about what makes you trust other people or what made you trust or distrust your parent when you were little. Here are a few tips that might help you to build trust with your child:

- **Be Consistent:** Children with ADHD often have difficulty trusting adults, especially if they have been let down in the past. It is important to be consistent with your expectations and consequences. This will help your child to know what to expect and will make it easier for them to trust you.

- **Be Honest:** If you make a promise to your child, be sure to keep it. If you can't keep a promise, explain why to your child and apologize. Own up to your mistakes by being honest about why it happened. Children are often more understanding than we might think.

- **Be Respectful:** Treat your child with respect, even when they are misbehaving. This means listening to them, avoiding name-calling and insults, and respecting their boundaries.

- **Be Supportive:** Let your child know that you are there for them and that you believe in them. Offer them help and support when they need it, but don't do everything for them. Encourage them to try their best and to learn from their mistakes.

- **Be Patient:** Building trust takes time and effort. Don't get discouraged if your child doesn't trust you right away. Just keep being consistent, honest, respectful, and supportive, and your child will eventually learn to trust you.

Building trust with a child with ADHD can be challenging, but it is worth it. When a child trusts their parents, they are more likely to listen to them, follow their guidance, and feel supported.

Teaching Problem-Solving Skills

As a parent, you need to teach your ADHD child the essential problem-solving skills of life. Teaching your ADHD child problem-solving skills can contribute to effective communication in several ways. First, it can help them to understand and express their own thoughts and feelings. When children know how to solve problems, they are better able to identify what is bothering them, come up with solutions, and communicate those solutions to others. Second, teaching your ADHD child problem-solving skills can help them to listen to and understand others. When children know how to solve problems, they are more likely to be open to hearing other people's perspectives and to working together to find solutions. Third, teaching your ADHD child problem-solving skills can help them to manage their emotions and behavior. When children know how to solve problems, they are less likely to react impulsively or to become overwhelmed by difficult situations.

Here are some tips for teaching your ADHD child problem-solving skills:

- **Brainstorming:** You can encourage your child to brainstorm solutions to the problem they're experiencing. There is often more than one way to solve a problem. Help your child to come up with as many possible solutions as they can.

- **Evaluation:** By helping your child to evaluate the solutions, they'll learn to weigh the pros and cons of each solution and choose the one that is most likely to work.

- **Implementation:** You should teach your child the importance of implementing the solution they've created. This may involve providing support and encouragement, since it can be quite a scary thing, especially if it involves conflict with others.

- **Celebrate Successes**: When your child solves a problem, be sure to praise them for their efforts. This will encourage them to repeat the process next time.

Resilience and Coping Strategies

Teaching your ADHD child coping strategies to manage frustration and stress can contribute to effective communication and building resilience in the following ways:

- improved emotional regulation

- reduced conflict

- increased self-confidence

Here are some coping strategies that you can teach your ADHD child to manage frustration and stress:

- **Deep Breathing:** Deep breathing is a simple but effective way to calm down and reduce stress. To teach your child deep breathing, have them sit in a comfortable position and place one hand on their chest and the other hand on their stomach. Have them take a slow, deep breath in through their nose, feeling their stomach expand. Then, have them exhale slowly through their mouth, feeling their stomach contract. Repeat this 5-10 times.

- **Relaxation Techniques:** Progressive muscle relaxation involves tensing and then relaxing each muscle group in the body. To teach your child progressive muscle relaxation, have them start by tensing and relaxing their toes. Then, have them move up their body, tensing and relaxing each muscle group in turn. Repeat this until you have reached the top of the head.

- **Time Management Skills:** Teach your child how to manage their time effectively. This will help them to stay on top of their work and reduce stress. To teach your child time management skills, help them to create a schedule and stick to it as much as possible. Also, teach them how to prioritize tasks and estimate how long each task will take..

- **Exercise:** Exercise is a great way to relieve stress and improve mood. Encourage your child to get regular exercise.

By teaching your ADHD child coping strategies to manage frustration and stress, you can help them to communicate more effectively, reduce conflict, and build resilience. These are all essential skills for success in life. At the end of the day, you want your child to feel free to come to you with anything and everything, but that won't happen on its own. You need to teach them these skills and also model it yourself. Clear and effective communication won't happen overnight, but this is a great place for you and your child to start. It's essential that you model resilience in everything you do, such as not giving up, always trying your best, and staying positive even when it feels like you've failed. Resilience is a key that every ADHDer needs in order to make a success of their life.

In the next chapter, we'll look at what to do when they don't behave the way they've been taught. How do you effectively discipline a child with ADHD without being too strict or too lenient with them? While we touched on some of these aspects in a previous chapter, the next chapter is dedicated to understanding and implementing positive discipline in order to manage ADHD behavior.

Chapter 5:

Positive Discipline and

ADHD Behaviors

A couple of years ago, I joined an online support group for parents with ADHD children. In the group, we shared with each other techniques that we found helpful, as well as our frustrations and victories. That's where I met Katie and Peter, and their 8-year-old, Alex. When we met, Alex frequently engaged in disruptive behavior, not only at school but also every other social event. It got to the point where Katie and Peter took turns going to church and staying home with Alex, since he would disrupt the entire service. Alex really struggled with managing his emotions and every time they went to the store, he would throw a tantrum, screaming and kicking at Katie. For a long time, Katie and Peter felt too bad for Alex to actually discipline him. They felt as if they were punishing him for something he couldn't control.

However, the other parents and professionals in the support group encouraged them to create a behavior management plan for Alex. The plan involved three different elements: behavior modification techniques, managing hyperactivity, and addressing inattention. After several weeks of implementing the behavior management plan, they started noticing a difference. He was less disruptive in class and in church, he followed instructions more clearly, and he even engaged in certain topics at school.

Even though every child is different, effective behavior management can help to transform challenging behavior. However, you need to modify and personalize the program so that it perfectly fits the needs of your ADHD child. In this chapter, we'll continue the conversation on positive reinforcements by taking it a step further and looking at other discipline methods that can be helpful for your child. We'll start by looking at behavior modification techniques, such as behavior charts and self-calming techniques that you can teach your child.

Behavior Modification Techniques

Behavior modification techniques are methods used to change a person's behavior. They are based on the principle that behavior is influenced by its consequences. By changing the consequences of a behavior, we can change the behavior itself. Behavior modification techniques can be used to change a wide range of behaviors, including both simple and complex ones. They are often used in schools, workplaces, and homes to help people learn new behaviors, reduce disruptive behaviors, and improve their overall functioning. Behavior modification techniques can be very effective in changing behavior, but it is important to use them responsibly and ethically. It is also important to note that behavior modification is not a quick fix. It takes time and effort to change behavior patterns.

One technique that is very helpful when it comes to behavior modification in young children with ADHD is using behavior charts.

Behavior Charts

Behavior charts are a type of behavior modification technique that can be used to help children with ADHD learn and practice appropriate behaviors. They work by providing children with a visual representation of their progress toward meeting specific behavioral goals. To create a behavior chart, first identify the specific behaviors that you want your child to work on which might include staying on task, following directions, raising their hand before speaking, or using kind words. Once you have identified the target behaviors, create a chart that lists each behavior and has a space for your child to earn a sticker or other reward for each time they demonstrate the desired behavior.

Once the chart is created, place it in a prominent location in your home where your child will see it often. At the beginning of each day, review the chart with your child and remind them of the target behaviors. Throughout the day, observe your child's behavior and praise them for each time they demonstrate a target behavior. At the end of the day, review the chart with your child again and give them a sticker or other reward for each target behavior that they met. Behavior charts can be a very effective tool for helping children with ADHD learn and practice appropriate behaviors. They are relatively easy to create and implement, and they can be used to target a wide range of behaviors.

Here are some tips for using behavior charts effectively:

- Choose a small number of target behaviors to focus on at a time.

- Make sure that the target behaviors are specific, measurable, achievable, relevant, and time-bound (SMART).

- Be consistent with using the behavior chart.

- Praise your child frequently for demonstrating the target behaviors.

- Use a variety of rewards that your child will find motivating.

- Make the behavior chart fun and engaging for your child.

- Be patient and understanding. It may take time for your child to learn and internalize the new behaviors.

Self-Calming Techniques

Another technique that is very helpful when it comes to behavior modification in young children with ADHD is teaching your child self-calming techniques. Self-calming techniques are behavior modification techniques that children with ADHD can use to manage their own emotions and behavior. These techniques can help children to reduce hyperactivity, impulsivity, and inattention. Some examples of helpful self-calming techniques include the following:

- **Mindfulness:** Mindfulness is the practice of paying attention to the present moment without judgment. This can help children to become more aware of their thoughts, feelings, and bodily sensations. Teach your child to focus on their breath or another repetitive task, such as counting their fingers or toes. If their mind wanders, have them gently bring their attention back to the original task.

- **Visualization:** Visualization involves using the power of imagination to create a calming and relaxing scene. Teach your child to imagine themselves in a place where they feel safe and happy. For example, they might imagine themselves lying on a beach, floating in a cloud, or playing in their favorite park.

- **Positive Self-Talk:** Positive self-talk involves challenging negative thoughts and replacing them with positive ones. Children with ADHD often have negative thoughts about themselves and their abilities. These thoughts can lead to feelings of anxiety, frustration, and anger. Positive self-talk can help children to change these negative thoughts and develop a more positive outlook of themselves.

- **Emotional Awareness:** Emotional awareness is the ability to identify and understand one's own emotions and the emotions of others. It is an important skill for everyone, but it can be especially helpful for children with ADHD. Emotional awareness can help children to better understand their emotions and to develop coping mechanisms for dealing with them in a healthy way.

Self-calming techniques can be taught to children of all ages, but it is important to start early. The more children practice these techniques, the better they will become at using them to manage their emotions and behavior.

If you don't know where to start when teaching your child these self-calming techniques, here's what I've found helpful:

- Start by teaching your child one technique at a time. Once they have mastered one technique, you can introduce another.

- Practice the techniques in a quiet and comfortable place.

- Make the practice fun and engaging. For example, you can turn deep breathing into a game or visualization into a story.

- Be patient and understanding. It may take time for your child to learn and use the techniques effectively.

Managing Hyperactivity

Managing hyperactivity as a part of positive discipline and behavior for children with ADHD involves using strategies that help children to channel their energy in a positive way and to learn to regulate their behavior. Helping your child manage their hyperactivity is important for various reasons:

- **Accidents:** Hyperactivity can sometimes lead to accidents and injuries. Children with ADHD are more likely to get into accidents than children without ADHD because they are often impulsive and have difficulty paying attention.

- **Interferes With Learning:** As we know, hyperactivity can interfere with learning. Children with ADHD often have difficulty sitting still and paying attention in class, which can make it difficult for them to learn and to succeed in school.

- **Relationship Issues:** Hyperactivity can cause problems with social relationships. Children with ADHD may have difficulty interacting with other children in a socially acceptable way. This is because they may be impulsive and have difficulty controlling their emotions.

So, how can we help them to manage their hyperactivity better without causing them to feel isolated or as if they are always in trouble? One of the best methods of managing hyperactivity is helping your child to channel their energy into something productive.

Channeling Energy Into Productive Outlets

Channeling energy into productive outlets is an effective way to manage hyperactivity in ADHD children. It helps them to burn off excess energy, improve their focus and attention, and develop new skills and interests at the same time. It is important to find productive outlets that your child enjoys and that are appropriate for their age and developmental level. It is also important to be supportive and to encourage your child to participate in the activities that they choose. There are three main outlets for hyperactivity:

- **Creative Outlet:** Creative activities can help children with ADHD to express themselves and to channel their energy in a positive way. Some ideas include painting, drawing, dancing, singing, and playing music.

- **Physical Outlet:** Children with ADHD need plenty of opportunities to be active. This can help to reduce their hyperactivity and improve their focus and attention. Encourage your child to participate in sports or other physical activities that they enjoy.

- **Social Outlet:** Social interaction can help children with ADHD to develop their social skills and to learn how to interact with others in a positive way. Look for opportunities for your child to socialize with other children, such as through sports teams, clubs, or playdates.

Another way that you can help your child focus their energy into a productive outlet is by encouraging them to find a hobby. Having a hobby can give children with ADHD a sense of purpose and can help them to develop their skills and interests. Encourage your child to try different hobbies until they find one that they enjoy.

Structured and Organized Environments

When your child struggles with hyperactivity, structured and organized environments are the way to go. I know that it might sound counterproductive, but being organized can actually help children who are hyperactive to calm down. There are three elements to creating a structured environment for your child with ADHD:

- **Clear Routines:** Clear routines are an important element of creating a structured environment to improve your ADHD child's hyperactivity. Children with ADHD thrive on structure and predictability. Routines can help them to know what to expect and to feel more in control. This can help to reduce their hyperactivity and improve their focus and attention. Start by creating a daily routine for them to follow which will include waking up, going to bed, eating meals, doing homework, chores, and playing. It is important to be flexible with the routine and to make adjustments as needed. For example, if your child is having a particularly difficult day, you may need to give them more time to do their homework or to play outside.

- **Visual Schedules:** We already briefly touched on visual schedules earlier on in this journey, but it's so helpful that it's worth mentioning again. Visual schedules are a great way to create a structured environment for children with ADHD. They help children to know what to expect throughout the day and to stay on task. To create a visual schedule, start by thinking about your child's daily routine. What activities do they do each day? In what order do they do them? Once you have identified your child's daily routine, you can start to create a visual schedule that represents it.

- **Organizational Aids:** Organizational aids are tools and strategies that can help children with ADHD to stay organized and to manage their hyperactivity. They can help children to keep track of their belongings, to plan and prioritize their work, and to stay on task. This includes tasks such as binders and folders, planners, checklists, labeling and color-coding, and timers and alarms. Organizational aids can be used to create a structured environment for children with ADHD, which can help to reduce their hyperactivity and improve their focus and attention.

Addressing Inattention and Focus Issues

It is important to address inattention and focus issues with your ADHD child because they can have a significant impact on their academic, social, and emotional development.

- **Academic Impact:** Children with ADHD often have difficulty paying attention in class, completing assignments on time, and taking tests. This can lead to poor academic performance and frustration.

- **Social Impact:** Children with ADHD may have difficulty interacting with other children in a socially acceptable way. This is because they may be impulsive and have difficulty controlling their emotions. This can lead to social isolation and problems with friendships.

- **Emotional Impact:** Children with ADHD may feel frustrated and discouraged by their difficulties with inattention and focus. This can lead to low self-esteem and depression.

For this section of the book, I want to specifically focus on the strategies that significantly improved my son's inattention and focus.

Improving Focus During Homework

Over the last couple of years, I've tried and tested loads of ways to improve focus during homework, some of which worked wonders, while others caused more chaos than anything else. However, the following five strategies truly helped me and my son to turn homework time around. While it used to be a time of anxiety, crying, and plenty of threats and disciplinary actions, it is now an organized time, part of the daily schedule.

- **Create Small Steps:** The first strategy is to break down tasks into smaller steps. Large tasks can be overwhelming for children with ADHD. Help your child to break down large tasks into smaller, more manageable steps. You can use checklists or to-do lists to help your child keep track of their progress.

- **Use Visual Cues:** Visual cues can help children with ADHD to stay organized and to follow directions. For example, you can use a timer to help your child stay on task, or you can use a color-coding system to organize their homework materials.

- **Make Homework Fun:** If your child finds homework boring, try to make it more fun by adding a game element or by doing their homework together.

- **Take Breaks:** Children with ADHD often have difficulty staying focused for long periods of time. Encourage your child to take breaks every 20-30 minutes to get up and move around, or to do something else that they enjoy.

- **Homework Routine**: The homework routine should include time for starting and finishing homework, as well as breaks. It is important to stick to the routine as much as possible.

If you're still struggling with homework time, remember to collaborate with others around you. Ask their teacher or perhaps therapist to give you guidelines on how to make homework time more effective and less dreadful.

Managing Distractions

Another way that you can help your child to improve their focus and attention is by managing the distractions around them. If you're not sure how to do that, here's a quick step-by-step guide to help your

ADHDer manage their distractions effectively without putting them in a bubble:

- **Identify Their Distractions:** The first step is to help your child identify what their distractions are. This can be done by keeping a journal or by simply talking to them about what tends to distract them. Once you know what their distractions are, you can start to develop strategies for helping them manage them.

- **Create a Distraction-Free Environment**: When your child is working on a task, try to create a distraction-free environment as much as possible. This means turning off the TV, putting away their phone, and finding a quiet place where they can work.

- **Set Realistic Expectations**: It is important to set realistic expectations for your child. Don't expect them to sit still and work on a task for hours on end. Instead, set shorter goals and break down tasks into smaller steps.

Positive discipline and managing ADHD behaviors can be a tricky topic to master, especially when your child doesn't respond to certain methods that your older children respond to. However, don't give up! Helping your child to adjust their behavior might take time, but I promise you that they'll appreciate and thank you for it later in life. Now that we have explored how to manage behavior and implement positive discipline, let's shift our focus to nurturing emotional well-being in children with ADHD.

Chapter 6:

Nurturing Emotional Well-Being

A couple of years ago, I got a phone call from my son's teacher, asking me to please come to the school as soon as possible. As I made my way there, I ran through all the scenarios in my mind, wondering which one it would be this time. Did he get up and walk around during the test period again? Or maybe he shot the teacher behind the head with his self-built catapult made from all the stationary in his backpack. I assumed that it was school-related, more specifically, academically related. So imagine my surprise when I got to school and saw the bruised eye on the boy sitting next to my son in the hallway. "He's not a fighter," I told his teacher, "This must have been a one-time thing." Unfortunately, it wasn't. Apparently, my sweet child, who I thought wouldn't hurt a fly, was growing into a bit of a bully. "But he told me that I was stupid!" my son argued as I explained his consequences to him. "It's not fair!" he screamed, kicking the car door. For the first time, I realized just how much he struggled with his emotions.

As parents, we often focus on the immediate needs, or the needs we can see. It's a rush to choose the right schools, implement the correct schedules, make sure that they're able to do well academically and get physical activity every day to help with the restless legs... and then we forget a little bit about the emotional side of things. While my son was doing better than ever academically, was the star of his baseball team, and was able to do all his chores without a meltdown, he was suffering emotionally. Right then and there, I knew that our next mission would be to help him nurture his emotional well-being.

In this chapter, we'll look at three aspects of nurturing emotional well-being in ADHD children:

- emotional intelligence

- anxiety and stress

- social skills and making friends

Children with ADHD experience emotions in a different way than other children. Things that would make neurotypical children mad might not bother your ADHDer at all. But other times, the opposite is true. While it wasn't nice of that child to call my son *stupid,* there were many other appropriate responses he could have chosen before jumping to hitting him in the face. So, we took some time, did some research, and started his journey to emotional well-being, the first stop being building emotional intelligence.

Building Emotional Intelligence

Emotional intelligence (EI) is the ability to identify, understand, and manage your own emotions, as well as the emotions of others. It is also the ability to use this information to guide your thoughts and behaviors (Ben Turkia et al., 2023). Emotional intelligence is an important skill that everyone should acquire, not just ADHDers, since it can help build and maintain strong relationships. Emotional intelligence can also help children to perform better at school, and adults to perform better at work. In order to manage stress and cope with all the difficulties that life might throw at you, you need to have emotional intelligence. This will also aid you to make better life decisions and achieve happiness and fulfillment. So, it begs the question: How can we help our ADHD children have higher emotional intelligence? Well, it's simple—we need to teach them emotional awareness and expression.

Teaching Emotional Awareness and Expression

Emotional awareness and expression is having the ability to understand what emotions you're experiencing and express them in an appropriate manner. For example, instead of punching his friend in the face, my son would've realized that he felt hurt by his friend and expressed that emotion with words instead. When you teach your child how to be aware of their own emotions, you are also encouraging them to have open dialogue with you. You show them how to have a safe space and how to use their words to express what they're feeling. In order to do so, your child needs to grow their emotional vocabulary. Have you ever felt *something* but you just couldn't find the word to express it? That might be due to a lack of emotional vocabulary, and for children with ADHD, that's called Tuesday. They have a hard time identifying emotions in general, so their vocabulary needs to be built up from scratch. For example, they can't tell you that they're disappointed in something if they don't know what it means to be disappointed. Here are a few ways that you can improve your child's emotional vocabulary:

- **Emotion Charades:** This is a fun and interactive game that can help your child to learn about different emotions. Have your child act out different emotions and see if you can guess what they are feeling. Then, take the opportunity to express an emotion to them and see whether they can identify it. That way, they'll start to notice how that emotion looks in others, as well as how it might feel within them.

- **Emotion Flashcards:** Show your child flashcards with different facial expressions and see if they can identify the emotion. You can also talk about what might cause someone to feel that way. By doing this, you will help them to understand that emotions are triggered by something else, which will help them to understand their own triggers as well.

- **Emotion Diary:** Encourage your child to keep an emotion diary. This can help them to track their emotions and learn more about what triggers them. Even if your child doesn't like writing, encourage them to write down one sentence every night to say how they're feeling or how their day went.

- **Emotion Check-Ins:** Throughout the day, ask your child how they are feeling. This can help them to stay in touch with their emotions and learn how to express them. If you see your child is starting to get overwhelmed with a certain emotion, take a second and chat them through it. Ask them what they're feeling and give them the opportunity to feel it in a safe environment.

Coping With Frustration and Disappointment

Frustration and disappointment are part of life and even though we want to protect our children from it, eventually they'll experience these negative emotions. Instead of trying to shelter your ADHD child from frustration or disappointment, rather help them to understand the emotions and teach them ways to cope with it. In previous chapters, we discussed problem-solving skills and teaching them to your child, which will be helpful when it comes to dealing with frustration and disappointment as well. You can also help your child by showing them healthy ways to manage their frustrations, like taking a deep breath or stepping away from the situation. It's important to remember that no matter what your child is feeling frustrated with or disappointed in, you need to provide them with validation and support. Here are some tips on how to teach your child with ADHD to cope with frustration and disappointment:

- **Acknowledge and Validate Their Feelings**: Let your child know that it's okay to feel frustrated and disappointed. Don't tell them to "stop being a baby" or to "just get over it." Instead, say something like, "I can see that you're feeling frustrated. It's okay to be upset."

- **Help Them to Identify Their Triggers**: What are the things that typically cause your child to feel frustrated or disappointed? Once you know what their triggers are, you can start to develop strategies for avoiding them or coping with them in a healthy way.

- **Teach Them Coping Skills**: There are many different coping skills that can help children with ADHD to manage their emotions. Some examples include deep breathing, muscle relaxation, and visualization. You can teach your child these coping skills and help them to practice using them in different situations.

Building emotional intelligence will take time and it will require a lot of encouragement and motivation. As you teach your child how to recognize their own emotions, you are also helping them to become more self-aware. You are teaching them to be mindful about their emotions, as well as the way that they respond to their emotions. Remember to always encourage your child to express their emotions, but to do so in a healthy way.

Addressing Anxiety and Stress

A big part of emotional well-being relies on stress and anxiety levels. A large number of children with ADHD also suffer from anxiety, and with all the social pressure these days on kids to be amazing at everything, many children leave the house every morning completely stressed. If you want your child to have good emotional well-being, you can't ignore the fact that they might be overwhelmed with stress and anxiety right now. The first step to helping your child deal with their anxiety is by recognizing their triggers.

Recognizing Triggers

It is important to help ADHD children identify their anxiety triggers for a number of reasons. First, it can help them to understand and manage their anxiety more effectively. When children know what triggers their anxiety, they can develop strategies for avoiding or coping with those triggers. This can help them to feel more in control of their anxiety and reduce their overall levels of stress and distress.

Second, identifying anxiety triggers can help ADHD children communicate their needs to others. For example, if a child knows that they are likely to feel anxious in large crowds, they can let their parents or teachers know so that they can take steps to accommodate them. This can help to reduce the child's anxiety and make them feel more comfortable in social situations. Third, identifying anxiety triggers can help ADHD children to make better choices. For example, if a child knows that staying up late at night triggers their anxiety, they can choose to go to bed earlier to reduce their risk of feeling anxious. This can help them to improve their sleep quality and overall mental and physical health.

Finally, identifying anxiety triggers can help ADHD children to develop resilience. When children know what triggers their anxiety and have strategies for coping with those triggers, they are better equipped to deal with challenges and setbacks. This can help them to build self-confidence and learn to persevere in the face of adversity. You can help your child to identify their triggers by using the following methods:

- **Talk It Through:** It's essential that you talk to your child about their anxiety. You can help them to identify and understand their anxiety symptoms, and what their triggers are. For example, you might say, "I notice that you start to feel anxious when you have to take a test. What are some of the things that make you feel anxious about tests?" By talking it through, you are teaching them to have the same kind of dialogue with themselves when they notice that they're feeling anxious.

- **Keep a Trigger Journal:** It is encouraged to have your child keep a journal of their anxiety symptoms and triggers. This can help them to identify patterns and start to predict when they are likely to feel anxious. You can also encourage them and remind them to write in their trigger journal when you notice that they've been triggered. If they're not sure what triggered it, chat through the situation with them and help them to pinpoint the trigger.

- **Use a Visual Scale:** You should help your child create a visual scale to track their anxiety levels. This can be a simple scale of 1 to 10, with 1 being the lowest level of anxiety and 10 being the highest. Have your child mark their anxiety level on the scale throughout the day, especially when they are feeling anxious.

- **Pay Attention to Your Child's Behavior**: Children with ADHD may express their anxiety in different ways, such as fidgeting, talking quickly, or avoiding certain situations. Pay attention to your child's behavior and try to identify any patterns or changes that may indicate that they are feeling anxious. If you understand their triggers better, you can help them to understand them as well.

Coping With Anxiety-Provoking Situations

Once the triggers are identified, it doesn't mean that they'll never experience an anxiety-provoking situation again. Instead, you should help them to cope with these types of situations which is important because anxiety can have a significant impact on their lives. It can make it difficult for them to focus in school, interact with peers, and participate in activities that they enjoy. By helping them to deal with anxiety-provoking situations, you're helping them to improve their overall well-being. One way that you can help your child to cope with anxiety-provoking situations is by making use of gradual exposure therapy.

Gradual exposure to anxiety triggers is a type of therapy that can help children with ADHD deal with anxiety-provoking situations. It involves gradually exposing the child to their anxiety triggers in a safe and controlled environment. This helps the child to learn how to manage their anxiety and cope with the situation without avoiding it. Gradual exposure to anxiety triggers is an effective treatment for anxiety disorders in children and adults. It is also a relatively safe and well-tolerated treatment. Here is an example of how gradual exposure to anxiety triggers might be used to help a child with ADHD who is afraid of dogs:

- The child might start by looking at pictures of dogs or watching videos of dogs.

- Once the child is comfortable with this, they might start by sitting in a room with a friendly dog that is behind a fence or gate.

- Gradually, the child would get closer to the dog until they are able to pet it and play with it.

Throughout the process, the child would be taught coping mechanisms for managing their anxiety, such as deep breathing and positive self-talk. However, remember to start with small steps. Don't try to expose your child to their biggest fear right away. Start with small steps and gradually work your way up. If they're scared of social events with loads of people, don't organize a surprise party for them where every person they know is present. Take it slow and keep to your child's pace. Don't rush through the process and keep encouraging them along the way. If you are struggling to help your child with gradual exposure to anxiety triggers on your own, don't be afraid to seek professional help. A therapist can guide you through the process and provide support for you and your child.

Stress-Reduction Techniques

To successfully and effectively deal with stress and anxiety, you need to help your child learn stress-reduction techniques. By teaching them stress-reduction techniques, you are helping them to manage their ADHD symptoms better and allowing them to take control over their own actions and thoughts. In earlier chapters, we discussed various ways to help your child deal with stress and manage their emotions, but if you need a quick recap, here are a couple of suggested activities to try:

- deep breathing

- progressive muscle relaxation

- visualization

- exercise

- spending time in nature

It is important to find stress-reduction techniques that work for your child and that they enjoy doing. You can help your child learn stress-reduction techniques by doing them together or by modeling them for your child. If you are struggling to help your child learn stress-reduction techniques on your own, don't be afraid to seek professional help. A therapist can teach your child stress-reduction techniques and provide support for you and your child.

Encouraging Social Skills and Peer Relationships

The final element of emotional well-being is helping your ADHDer to have positive peer relationships, which will require some good social skills. Positive peer relationships are important for all children, but they are especially important for children with ADHD. Children with ADHD often have difficulty making and keeping friends. This can be due to a number of factors, such as their hyperactivity, impulsivity, and difficulty paying attention. However, positive peer relationships can have a number of benefits for children with ADHD, including:

- **Improved Self-Esteem:** You might have noticed that your ADHDer often has low self-esteem due to their social difficulties. Positive peer relationships can help them to feel better about themselves and their abilities. It's important that they have friends who they feel understand and accept them.

- **Reduced Loneliness and Isolation:** Children with ADHD are prone to feeling lonely and isolated due to their social difficulties. Positive peer relationships can help them to feel connected to others and reduce their feelings of loneliness and isolation.

- **Improved Social Skills.** Since children with ADHD often have difficulty with social skills, positive peer relationships can help them to learn and practice social skills in a safe and supportive environment. By having friends to interact with, they'll learn how to behave socially.

Parents and caregivers can play an important role in helping children with ADHD to develop positive peer relationships. Let's start by looking at how to navigate the social challenges that your ADHDer might run into.

Navigating Social Challenges for Children With ADHD

Many children who are neurodivergent find socializing with others a little tricky. While some make friends quickly, they might struggle to maintain the friendships long-term. As a parent, you might wonder how you can navigate these social challenges and help your child to have friends. Chances are, you're thinking about it more than they are, but that doesn't mean that we shouldn't help them. Children with ADHD desperately want to make friends and be liked by others, but they're often unsure how to express that to others. The good news is that you can do something about it (without being the parent that meddles too much). There are three ways that you can help your child navigate social challenges (Low, 2019):

- **Increase Their Awareness:** Step one is to increase their social awareness. Since children with ADHD are often unaware of those around them, they need to learn that their actions affect those around them. In some cases, they might leave a conversation thinking that it went well, when in reality, it didn't. You can help your child be aware of others' feelings by explaining to them how others might perceive their behavior and encouraging them to think about it as well.

- **Practice:** The next step is to practice, practice, practice. Previously, we talked about using role playing or charades to understand emotions, and the same technique can be used here. The more they practice understanding and interacting with others, the more they'll understand other people.

- **Create Opportunities:** Finally, you need to create opportunities for them to be social and test their new skills. Whether it's by taking them to the park or organizing a playdate, it's essential that you provide opportunities outside of the school environment.

Promoting Positive Friendships

There are very few things as heartbreaking as seeing your child struggle to make friends. So, what can we do? How can we guide them toward positive friendships without receiving eyerolls from our kids? Well, there are a couple of ways in which we, as the parents, can help them find friends that will have a positive influence on them (Edelman, 2006):

- **Follow Their Interests:** If your child has a specific interest in something, allow them to pursue it and find friends who also have the same love or interest. For example, if your child is into Minecraft, look for other video-game fans that would be a good friend for your child. A shared interest will help your child to feel confident and engaged in the social interaction.

- **One-on-One Playmates:** Playdates are essential for child development, but since ADHD children tend to be more competitive than others, when it's a group of three, they might feel excluded or ganged up on. So, start with one-on-one playdates and take it from there.

- **Seek Younger Friends:** ADHDers might be a little less mature than other children their age, and they are often very aware of that fact. So, why not look for friends a couple of years younger than them? That way, your child won't feel left behind or intimidated to have a conversation.

- **Keep It Short:** When hosting a playdate, keep it short. ADHDers get tired of their companions quickly and it can lead to being irritable or being rude to their friends, throwing a spanner in the wheel. Keep the playdate short and sweet, before things can go sour.

- **Set an Example:** You can't expect your child to have all the friends in the world when they never see you interact with your own friends. Be sure that you talk about your own friendships in front of the children, as well as invite them over for tea (or wine). When your child sees how you interact with your friends, they'll start to mimic that behavior.

Understanding Personal Space

Children with ADHD often struggle to understand personal space. This can be because they're simply too excited to pay attention to others' social cues, or perhaps because they forget that other people have their own personal needs. If you want your child to be socially successful, there are a few things that you can do to help them understand personal space:

- **Explain:** You should start by explaining the concept of personal space in a way that your child can understand. You can use a visual aid, such as a hula hoop, to demonstrate how much space people need around them. You can also talk about how everyone has different personal space needs, and what it feels like when someone gets too close.

- **Practice:** Play games where your child has to stay a certain distance away from you or another person in order for them to understand the concept of distance. You can also practice social skills groups or playdates with other children who are learning about personal space.

- **Consistency:** Let your child know that it is important to respect other people's personal space, and remind them of this rule when necessary. If something wasn't allowed yesterday, make sure that it's also not allowed today. My ADHD son used to tease his little sister by licking her cheeks. While it was funny at first, we had to be consistent with telling him that it wasn't allowed and that he was invading her personal space.

- **Reminders:** Be patient, but remind them constantly of what it means to respect others' personal space. If you see them cross a line with friends or family, speak up and address the behavior immediately. This will help them start to notice their mistakes on their own.

By helping your child nurture emotional well-being, you are one step closer to understanding your child fully and helping them to succeed. Even though change won't happen overnight, it's essential that you start sooner rather than later to avoid them growing up and feeling incompetent. Now that we have discussed emotional well-being, let's explore strategies to support academic success for children with ADHD.

Chapter 7:

Fostering Academic Success

Every human on this earth has different abilities, strengths, and weaknesses. Being an academic isn't for everyone, that much is true. However, whether you want to be a rocket scientist or a stand-up comedian, there is some sort of academic success required. We don't know what our children will be when they grow up. That's up to them to decide when they're a little older and wiser. But it's our job as parents to help them be successful and achieve their full potential. Academic success doesn't only mean achieving straight As. For your child, it might mean going to school every day and paying attention in class. No matter what we deem as "success," it's our job as the parents to foster academic success to some degree within our ADHD children.

Fostering academic success in your ADHD child is important for a number of reasons. First, it can help them to reach their full potential and to achieve their goals. Second, it can help them to develop the skills and knowledge they need to be successful in college and the workforce. Third, it can help them to build self-esteem and confidence. So, how do we do it? How can we help our children academically without taking over or putting too much pressure on them? There are a couple of elements to fostering academic success, including

- creating the perfect learning environment for your child specifically.

- approaching homework with a strategy.

- cultivating a love for learning.

In this chapter, we'll look at these three elements and how we as the parents can help our children to achieve academic success by embracing their own way of doing things.

Tailoring Learning Environments

In an earlier chapter, we discussed setting up a specific space for your ADHDer so that they can do their homework in an organized and prepared space. Now, it's time to take a closer look. In order to tailor a learning environment, you first need to understand your child's needs and learning style.

Understanding Your Child's Learning Style

I absolutely love the Albert Einstein quote that says, "Everybody is a genius. But if you judge a fish by its ability to climb a tree, it will live its whole life believing that it is stupid." In many ways, it sums up the societal pressure and misconceptions regarding children with ADHD. When I was a little girl, I had a best friend who had ADHD, but he never got diagnosed professionally. Unfortunately, our teacher didn't see ADHD as "real" and used it as an excuse to point out my friend's flaws and struggles. She would often call him out in front of the whole class, saying that he was lazy or unintelligent. She sometimes would go so far as to say things like, "You'll never be successful," or "See you again next year, in this same class." I remember how I would go home and cry to my mom, heartbroken that the teacher would be so mean to my friend (In retrospect, that's probably why I didn't trust my son's teacher at first). My friend was a fish, judged on his ability to climb a tree. Today, he runs a very successful crafting business, where he makes personalized and unique furniture pieces that are absolutely beautiful! He is successful, because he is doing what he is good at—working with his hands.

In order to avoid judging our little fish by their ability to climb a tree, we need to understand that children have different learning styles, and when we're able to help them fully embrace those, they'll achieve success much more easily. By embracing their learning style, we'll help the fish to swim and not force it to climb.

There are seven different learning styles (Brain Balance Centers, n.d.):

- **Physical (kinesthetic):** This is the most common learning style for children with ADHD. With this learning style, the child will prefer to use their hands, body, and sense of touch to learn.

- **Verbal (linguistic):** This style of learning involves speech and writing. It's also quite common among ADHDers.

- **Solitary (intrapersonal):** In this learning style, the child prefers to work on their own and not with others around them.

- **Social (interpersonal):** When a child has this style of learning, they learn best when they're surrounded by others or studying in groups.

- **Logical (mathematical):** With this learning style, children use systems, reasoning, and logic to learn.

- **Aural (auditory-musical):** This type of learning style involves the child making use of music and sound to learn new information.

- **Visual (spatial):** If a child is a visual learner, they prefer using spatial understanding, images, and pictures.

Take a moment to observe your child's natural learning ability. Do they tend to speak to themselves when learning something (verbal)? Do they make more progress when a sibling or a friend is doing homework with them (social)? Perhaps they're spinning around on their chair as they're memorizing new information (physical)? By taking note of this, you'll start to understand their learning style and be able to support them better, preparing the environment to be set up for that specific learning style.

Creating an ADHD-Friendly Study Environment

Every learning style has different needs and elements that will work well. The best way to embrace your child's learning style is by setting up the space to best suit their preferences. Let's have a look at what an ideal study environment might look like for every learning style.

Physical (Kinesthetic)

To set up a study spot for a kinesthetic learner, you should focus on creating a space where they can move around and be active. Here are a couple things you can consider adding to their space:

- **Choose a Large Space:** Kinesthetic learners need room to move around, so it is important to choose a large study space. This could be a spare bedroom, a basement, or even a backyard.

- **Provide Plenty of Seating Options:** Kinesthetic learners may need to change their seating position frequently, so it is important to provide them with plenty of options. This could include a chair, a beanbag chair, a floor pillow, or even a standing desk.

- **Add Some Movement to the Study Space:** You can add some movement to the study space by placing a whiteboard or chalkboard in the space, or by providing your child with some fidget toys. You can also encourage your child to take breaks to move around, stretch, or do some light exercise.

- **Make the Space Comfortable and Inviting:** The study space should be a place where your child feels comfortable and relaxed. This means making sure that the space is well-lit and has a comfortable temperature. You may also want to allow your child to decorate the space in their own personal style.

Verbal (Linguistic)

In order to set up a space for your child with a verbal style of learning, it's essential that they're in a space where they can properly hear themselves and feel confident enough to speak out loud. Many children might feel self-conscious about learning out loud, so make sure that they have a safe space. You can also encourage them to record their study work and listen to it during the day to help them retain the information better.

- **Choose a Quiet Location:** Verbal learners need to be able to concentrate on what they are hearing or reading, so it is important to choose a study location that is as quiet as possible.

- **Minimize Distractions:** Remove any potential distractions from the study space, such as televisions, computers, and video games. It is also important to close any doors or windows that may lead to noise or visual distractions.

- **Provide the Necessary Supplies:** Make sure that your child has all of the supplies they need to study, such as pencils, pens, paper, and textbooks. You may also want to provide them with a whiteboard or chalkboard so that they can brainstorm ideas and visualize concepts.

- **Encourage Your Child to Talk About What They Are Learning:** Verbal learners learn best by talking about what they are learning. Encourage your child to talk to you, a friend, or a study partner about what they are learning. You can also ask them questions to help them to process the information.

- **Help Your Child to Develop Good Note-Taking Skills:** Good note-taking skills are essential for verbal learners. Help your child to develop good note-taking skills by teaching them how to identify the main points of a lecture or reading passage, and how to summarize the information in their own words.

Solitary (Intrapersonal)

Since solitary learners require solitude in order to study effectively, you need to set up a space for them where no one can interrupt them. Setting up an ideal study spot for a solitary or intrapersonal learner involves creating a space that fosters focus, reflection, and personal exploration. Here are some key considerations for establishing a conducive learning environment for this type of learner:

- **Location:** Choose a quiet and distraction-free area where the learner can concentrate without interruptions. A dedicated study room, a secluded corner of the house, or even a peaceful spot in nature can be suitable options.

- **Technology:** Provide access to necessary technology, since they might look for answers online instead of wanting to ask a friend. Technology can include devices such as a computer, tablet, or study apps, while minimizing potential distractions from social media or non-academic websites. Consider using productivity tools or website blockers to maintain focus.

- **Sensory Preferences:** Cater to the learner's sensory preferences. If they prefer silence, ensure the space is quiet and free from noise disruptions. If they prefer background sounds, provide options for calming music, nature sounds, or white noise.

Social (Interpersonal)

Social learners learn best when they are in a group, but this can sometimes be tricky to manage, since the social aspect can also lead to distractions. Setting up an effective study spot for an ADHD child who is a social-style learner requires a multifaceted approach that caters to their unique learning preferences and needs where they get to be social, but can also remain focused.

- **Study Groups:** A great way to help a social learner is by setting up study groups. A good friend of mine has a child with ADHD who thrives when she's socializing and able to study with friends. So, my friend started a homework center where kids can come after school and do their homework, either on their own or in a group. That way, her daughter is always surrounded by others when she's doing homework or studying, without the constant distraction of other friends or the possibility of doing something else instead.

- **Communal Space:** While most of the other study types require isolation and a quiet room to work in, social learners thrive in a communal space. However, the space should still be free of distractions. For example, if your children are doing homework around the kitchen table, make sure the radio or television isn't on to distract them. Being surrounded by others doesn't mean there's no order or no sense of focus.

- **Rewards:** If your child is studying with a friend or perhaps another sibling, reward them with some social time. For example, if they've been studying for 20 minutes, allow them to then chat about other things for 5 minutes before jumping back in. These frequent rewards of social interaction will help them to remain motivated and focused on the work.

Logical (Mathematical)

Logical learners are usually very methodical and they think in a linear order. That's why their study space needs to be a space where they can feel inspired, motivated, and interested in the topic at hand. They'll often want to write, draw, or even make models in order to understand certain concepts. You can prepare a space for them by including the following elements:

- **Desk:** While some other learners prefer sitting on a comfortable couch or perhaps on the floor (or not sitting at all), logical learners need a space with a big desk where they can write, draw, or create their own visual aids when they're trying to understand a concept. Make sure that the desk is big enough for them not to feel frustrated by their own creations.

- **Computer:** Logical learners might require the usage of a computer earlier on in their lives than other learners—that's because they might want to research statistics or analytical programs as part of their normal study process. They don't just want to learn facts, but they want to understand where these facts come from.

- **Supplies:** Logical learners might find different supplies extremely helpful when they're studying. One of the best ways to incorporate that into their study material is by having a certain set of Legos or blocks that are dedicated to their study area. Encourage them to use those supplies to then build models to better understand the concept at hand.

Aural (Auditory-Musical)

When a child is an aural learner, they tend to grasp concepts regarding music and rhythm much faster than others. They can also process sound in a different way than others can, helping them to process information that they hear more easily than information that they see. People with musical learning styles require a study spot that allows them to make use of their musical skills.

- **Speaker and Recorder:** When aural learners hear something, they are more likely to remember the information. That's why their study spot should include a speaker and a recorder where they can listen to information as well as record information that they can later relisten to.

- **Freedom:** Even if you're not an aural learner, you need to provide your child encouragement and safety to use their musical abilities. One way that you can do that is by helping them write jingles containing the information they need to learn. This might feel silly, but many aural learners transform their study material into a rap or a song in order to remember it better.

- **Musical Instruments:** Since aural students respond positively to different rhythms, you can include some musical instruments in their study room. While they're studying, they might use a small drum to bash on as they're memorizing longer materials. By creating the rhythm, they will hear and feel the study material and have a better chance at recalling it later.

- **Performance:** Many children might be self-conscious about this type of learning style, since it might seem unconventional. Embrace it by encouraging your child to put on a concert for you and the rest of the family after a study session. This will not only make them more comfortable with their learning style, but it will also give them the opportunity to repeat what they've learned, cementing the information even further into their minds.

Visual (Spatial)

The last type of learning that we should discuss is visual learning. A visual learner has the ability to perceive, analyze, and understand visual information around them. They see everything as pictures and graphs and remember that more easily than when they hear something. They often tend to overlook small details in order to see the bigger picture. To set up a learning space for a visual learner, you need to consider a couple of things:

- **Supplies:** A visual learner needs to make use of their learning style by drawing and creating their own pictures that will help them remember the content. For example, if they're studying history, they might draw the battle they're learning about in order to retain the information instead of simply saying the dates out loud. Make sure that their space has enough supplies for them to use when drawing or creating their masterpieces.

- **Study Wall:** While art on walls can often distract other learning types, you should encourage your child to put their study drawings on the wall. That way, they can look at them every day and remember what they're studying. For example, if they're learning about the human skeleton, allow them to draw and stick the different parts of the skeleton onto their wall. Then, as they learn the smaller details, they can add sticky notes or some other pictures to the different parts of the skeleton, until the entire picture is visible.

- **Stories:** Another way that they can study effectively is by making up stories about the content they're learning. Since stories are also visual, they'll have a better chance at remembering the content when it's set up in a creative way or in a storytelling way. For example, if they're learning about evolution, encourage them to create a story in their mind where a character is going through the different stages of evolution, helping them to remember each stage more clearly and effectively.

By embracing the different learning styles, you're helping your child to be successful and achieve academic success. This doesn't mean that they'll suddenly have straight As, but it does mean that they'll be less frustrated, more motivated, and more confident in their own abilities. This will also help them to cultivate a love for learning, instead of dreading it.

Cultivating a Love for Learning

Besides what we might think, children gravitate toward learning. Why else would they be so interested in the zoo and the aquarium, or even the museums with ships and dinosaurs? It's because they are wired to *want* to learn. Yet, when it comes to school, they are often bored or very uninterested in learning, probably because they don't understand what they're learning or why it's important. When it comes to dinosaurs and airplanes, it's easy to be interested because it's something they use when they're playing or drawing. But remember, facts from the Cold War might not be so exciting to learn. As parents, we need to help our children grow and learn by cultivating a love for learning from a young age, and it all starts by encouraging curiosity.

Encourage Curiosity

When you tell a child you have something to teach them, they will most likely push back. Why? Because they weren't curious about the topic first. Instead, you have to make them curious about something and then sneak in the lessons you want them to learn. Encouraging curiosity in an ADHD child involves fostering a supportive environment that nurtures their natural inquisitiveness and provides opportunities for exploration and discovery. Here are some strategies to consider:

Embrace Their Questions: Encourage your child to ask questions, no matter how silly or outlandish they may seem. Show genuine interest in their inquiries and engage in open discussions. Even if the question is something along the lines of, "Do mermaids exist?" lean into the question and help them to be further curious. You can either point them in the direction of mythology, researching mermaids and learning more about them. Or, it might go in the direction of the ocean and how there are many things we don't know about it. Either way, that question can lead to other questions, so embrace and encourage their curiosity.

Provide Hands-On Experiences: Engage your child in hands-on activities that allow them to explore their interests and discover new things. Experiments, nature walks, building projects, and creative pursuits can spark curiosity. You should also encourage exploration while you're at it. Provide opportunities for your child to explore their surroundings and interests. Visit museums, parks, libraries, or attend workshops and events that align with their passions.

Embrace Mistakes and Failures: Encourage your child to view mistakes and failures as learning opportunities. Help them understand that setbacks are part of the learning process and can lead to new discoveries. You should also show your own curiosity and enthusiasm for learning. Share your interests with your child, take them on adventures, and demonstrate the joy of discovery.

Create a Curiosity-Friendly Environment: Surround your child with books, puzzles, games, and other stimulating materials that encourage exploration and discovery. Allow your child to take the lead in their learning journey. Follow their interests, support their initiatives, and provide resources to fuel their curiosity.

Above all, remember to celebrate their curiosity. Recognize and praise your child's inquisitiveness and show them that their curiosity is valued and encourage them to continue exploring and learning. Remember, curiosity is a powerful motivator for learning. By fostering a supportive and stimulating environment, you can help your ADHD child develop a lifelong love of learning and discovery.

Academic Achievements

Another way that you can cultivate a love for learning is by celebrating their academic success. No matter how small or big the improvement is, celebrate it wholeheartedly. This will encourage your child to keep trying. Even if they don't make progress academically with their marks but they've been better at remaining focused and causing less disruptions, celebrate it! Their academic achievements can also be celebrated with rewards or special activities to show them how proud you are of them and that it's not something you're overlooking. Another way to celebrate academic achievements is by involving the rest of the family in the celebration. By fostering a love for learning and providing positive reinforcement, you can help your child to develop a mindset of growth and a passion for education. All of this will help your child to enjoy school and not dread every second.

As we conclude our exploration of emotional intelligence and well-being, it's time to pivot toward another crucial aspect of your child's ADHD journey: managing transitions and challenges. Just as a skilled sailor adjusts their course when facing changing winds, our next chapter will equip you with strategies to help your child navigate the seas of transitions and overcome the challenges that lie ahead.

Chapter 8:

Managing Transitions and Challenging Changes

Change can have a big impact on everyone. Many of the things we as adults fear the most all come down to the fear of change and what the unknown might bring. Since ADHD children find comfort and peace within routine, they can struggle with change quite significantly. Whether a small change or something major, you can help your ADHDer through it and learn to manage your stress better as well. In this chapter, we'll look at the various ways in which you can help your ADHD child through transitions and challenging changes. The first thing we need to prepare for is helping our children cope with different kinds of transitions.

Coping With Transitions

Transitions are part of life and they're unavoidable. Even in school, you're constantly transitioning between classes, teachers, and year groups. This can trigger some serious ADHD symptoms, causing your child to struggle with behavior they can usually manage well. I know by now that during the first term of every year, my son's behavior is at its worst. He constantly disrupts classes and he tends to struggle academically. But as he adjusts, so does his behavior. However, over the years, I've learned how to help him prepare for change, making the transition easier for him to manage.

Preparing for Change

In order to prepare your ADHDer for change, you first need to let them know that change is happening. You can't fully prepare someone for something by pretending that it doesn't exist. That's why the first step of preparing for change requires you to provide advance notice of the upcoming change, whether in routine or the environment. Give your child enough time to adjust by giving them visual aids. For example, let them know in advance that they might be having to go to bed sooner in a month, and set up a visible countdown calendar for them to take note of. In this way, they can anticipate the change more effectively. You should also offer reassurance and support during these times of change, emphasizing the positive aspects of the new situations at hand. For example, let them know that going to bed earlier is a good thing because that means they'll feel more rested in the morning and will be able to get up and have a run with you before school. You can prepare them for the change by listing both the pros and the cons, which will help them to understand what's happening much better.

School Transitions

One of the biggest transitions that they might have to face as a child is school transitions, especially when they're moving to middle school from elementary school. There are a couple of ways that you can aid in this transition period of their lives:

- **Visits:** Before it's time to go to school, make sure that you and your ADHDer go and visit the new school together. Help your child to familiarize themselves with their surroundings and be sure to point out the positive things that you're noticing.

- **Meet the Teachers:** Make sure to arrange a meeting with their primary teacher and allow your child to meet them before school starts. That little bit of familiarity will help them to be at ease and understand what's happening a little bit better.

- **Communicate:** It's essential that you encourage your child to voice their thoughts openly. Whether they're scared or excited, make sure that they understand that you're there for them and that feeling these emotions isn't wrong or against the rules.

- **Friends:** Ask around and identify which of your child's friends might also be transitioning to the same school. Have a special playdate where you encourage them to talk about the new school to ensure that they have a special bond regarding school. Having a friend there will help your child to not feel like a fish out of water.

Major Event Changes

When it comes to major events, your child might need some additional support. Certain major events can't be pre-planned, but there are other ways that you can help your child through events such as moving or divorce.

- **Dialogue:** Instead of simply telling your child what is happening, make them part of the conversation. If you're moving to a new house, ask them what they think about the new kitchen or perhaps which room they would like to live in. Encouraging them to join the dialogue will help them to feel less out of control.

- **Consistency:** Even though certain things will change, other things will remain the same. It's your job to help your child identify the things that will remain consistent. A good example of this in the case of a divorce is to let your child know that even though big change is coming, both parents will never stop loving them.

By proactively preparing and supporting your child during life transitions, you can help them navigate these changes with greater ease and minimize the stress associated with new environments or major life events.

Addressing Co-Occurring Conditions

ADHD often co-occurs with other conditions such as depression and anxiety. When this happens in your child, there are three things that you should consider and keep in mind at all times.

Understanding and Managing

As a parent, you need to be aware of the symptoms of comorbid conditions that may accompany ADHD. You need to know which symptoms are ADHD-related, and which symptoms are something else. You should consult a professional or perhaps read up on the different symptoms of comorbid conditions. Once you do and you've noticed that your child is showing symptoms other than what they usually do, you can move on to the second element that you need to consider.

Seek Treatment

If your child is showing symptoms of anxiety or depression, you should consider seeking treatment for them. These kinds of conditions very rarely go away on their own, and you have to help your child through it. Research and explore available treatment options for the conditions, such as therapy, counseling, or perhaps a support group. Once you've done your research, be sure to speak to your child about it and ask them whether they're feeling differently than usual and what they might think the matter is. Don't forget to rely on teachers and other professionals when your child needs the additional support. You should also educate yourself on the co-occurring conditions in order to better understand your child's needs and experiences. These kinds of conditions don't have to become unbearable or cause you and your child to drift apart from one another.

The Impact of Medication

The third element you need to consider is medication. There are many medications out there that might help your child, but some of the medications also come with their own side effects. Be sure to speak to a professional in order to understand the options you and your child have. When you decide on a medication, you need to monitor your child closely and clearly communicate the changes they might be expressing to the healthcare provider. When you are concerned that their depression or anxiety might be getting worse, communicate it to your healthcare provider before changing the dosage on your own. It's essential to understand that ADHD medication can help manage certain symptoms, but that doesn't mean that it's a cure-all solution.

By addressing co-occurring conditions alongside ADHD and seeking appropriate treatment and support, you can provide a comprehensive and holistic approach to your child's overall well-being and development.

Handling Behavioral Crisis

When a crisis hits, it can be really difficult for children with ADHD to manage their emotions. Fear might become overwhelming or they might feel completely confused by the challenges they're facing. Luckily, you can help your ADHDer through a crisis or a traumatic experience by de-escalating the situation.

De-Escalation Techniques

When you're de-escalating a situation, the first thing you need to do is remain calm. If you're panicking and unable to remain composed, your child most definitely won't be able to. You need to model a calm and composed form to promote self-control to your child. When speaking to them, instead of being panicked, make sure that you use a calm voice that will reassure your child that everything will be okay. When communicating with them, avoid confrontation. Instead, encourage your child to take a couple of deep breaths and do whatever you can to help them to calm down. Once they're calm, you can start an open dialogue about what happened or what they experienced.

Strategies for Safety

It's essential that you have a crisis management plan at hand at all times, whether at school or at home. A crisis management plan consists of clear steps on what to do when there's an emergency. For example, when your child is experiencing a meltdown at school, their teacher should be aware of the strategy that you have in place for when something like that usually happens. The plan needs to be specific and outline every step that is required. For example:

- Remove the child from the classroom and allow them to be in a different room where they have privacy.

- Remove distractions and make sure that the room isn't brightly lit and that there's no other sound to overwhelm them.

- Offer a glass of water and encourage them to do their breathing exercises.

- Call mom or dad to update on what happened.

- Allow the child to rest on their own for a while before returning to class.

Be sure to communicate the crisis plan to all teachers, caregivers, and perhaps even the parents of their close friends who they might have playdates with.

Part of the safety plan should also include rules and expectations so that your child doesn't start exploiting the system. Be sure to establish clear rules and to communicate these rules to others as well. You should also notify other parents and teachers about possible triggers that might cause your ADHDer to experience a crisis. The goal isn't to encourage everyone to walk on eggshells around your child and avid triggers at all costs, but rather to help them understand what your child might be experiencing in that exact moment.

When my son went to middle school, he experienced a lot of change. He started carpooling with other moms, he had a whole new school to get used to, and the way things worked at his new school were very different than what he was used to. One of the things that really helped him to manage his emotions was listening to music. So, when he had an overwhelming day, he would often put on his headphones and not talk to the other friends or moms. At first, some of the moms thought he was a little bit rude, but after I explained to them that it was him managing his emotions, they understood and allowed him to have his space. At school, he would often feel the need to move his legs or move while being in a class. As any ADHDer would tell you, having restless legs can be excruciating and no matter how hard you try to keep still, it's an overwhelming feeling. After explaining this to the teachers, they agreed that he would be allowed to stand up during class and march on the spot or stretch when he felt the need to, if he didn't disrupt the class. So, he would often stand up, walk to the back of the class and do stretches while listening to what the teacher had to say. These simple methods help him on a daily basis to manage his symptoms better, while dealing with the changes.

By implementing de-escalation techniques, creating crisis management plans, and prioritizing safety and emotional well-being, you can effectively manage behavioral crises and provide support during challenging moments for your child with ADHD. By nurturing a positive attitude toward setbacks and failures and promoting emotional strength, you can help your child develop a resilient and emotionally healthy mindset as they navigate the challenges of living with ADHD.

Chapter 9:

Social Skills and Peer Relationships

ADHD should never be used as an excuse for your child to be rude or act in a way that can hurt others. Sure, emotional and social skills might not come as easily to children with ADHD than those without, but that doesn't mean that your child can't be kind, compassionate, and empathetic toward their friends. When we use ADHD as an excuse for bad behavior or children acting in a way that's rude or inappropriate, we subconsciously teach our children that they can do whatever they want because they have ADHD. The lesson we should be teaching is that despite their ADHD, they are still positive, kind, and polite children. As parents, we can help our ADHDers to achieve good social skills and manage positive peer relationships, without compromising or changing who they are. We can do this by teaching them the necessary social skills they need, by encouraging empathy and understanding for others and not just for themselves, and by helping them learn how to build positive friendships. That's exactly what we'll be exploring in this chapter, starting with teaching them the basic social skills required.

Teaching Social Skills

One of the best ways to learn something is by doing it over and over again until you've mastered it. It's the same when it comes to social skills—the more you practice, the better you'll be at it. Practicing social skills can be a little tricky, which is why you need to engage in roleplaying and social scripts with your ADHDer. When you engage in roleplay scenarios at home, you help your child to practice common social situations such as introductions and joining a group conversation. Roleplaying will allow you the opportunity to provide your child feedback and constructive guidance on how to interact with others. By encouraging them and teaching them how to engage, you're boosting their confidence and helping them to feel empowered to do it in real situations. "Social scripts" refers to a set of general rules or options that you can use when in conversation. This includes things like asking "How are you?" when seeing someone for the first time that day, or repeating the question back at them when asked something interesting. Social scripts will help your child to have prepared phrases to make use of during the initial parts of the conversation.

Practicing Social Interactions

Practicing social interactions might sound a little strange at first, but you don't have to overthink it. Just play with your child as you would normally, but take note of their social behavior. You can also encourage them to interact more or perhaps express how something they did made you feel. Engaging in roleplay will help your child to understand what is expected of him or her when in a social environment, such as introducing themselves to a group. As you engage in roleplay, provide positive feedback and constructive guidance to help boost your child's confidence. When they feel like they're doing a good job, they'll be more eager to try it out with others. Before your child enters a social situation, be sure to encourage them to remember the scripts and roleplaying. Being reminded of what they learned right before a social interaction will help them to use what they practiced and use it to imitate the conversations. A big part of practicing social interactions should be devoted to helping your child understand social cues better.

Understanding Social Cues

ADHD children might have a hard time picking up on social cues, so it's up to you to teach them how to read a room and pick up on nonverbal communication.

You can help your child to understand social cues by looking at body language, facial expressions, and tone of voice.

- **Body Language:** Body language accounts for almost 65% of all communication, which means that if your child doesn't understand body language, they might miss a lot of information. Body language includes posture, gestures, and movements, and body language can help us to understand what others are really feeling (Cherry, 2023). You can help your child to pick up on body language by making use of visual aids or by pointing out certain body language that they might be missing.

- **Facial Expressions:** A person can convey a lot with their face and it can either express real feelings, or hide what we're actually feeling deep down (Cherry, 2023). It's important to understand facial expressions, since it can help you determine whether someone is telling the truth or not. In fact, according to research, we often make judgments about peoples' intelligence based on their faces and expressions (Cherry, 2023).

- **Tone of Voice:** The tone of your voice can say a lot more than the words you're communicating. If I say, "Wow, so exciting!" in an uplifting, joyful tone, you'll probably believe that I truly find what you just told me really exciting. However, if I say, "Wow, so exciting," with a monotone voice, you'll probably pick up the sarcasm. We need to help our ADHD children to be able to pick up on those tone changes in order to help them identify people's real motives. You can do so by watching movies together and examining the different tones of the characters or by taking turns to change your tone of voice to say something else.

Navigating Conversations

When engaging with your child, you can also incorporate important lessons such as taking turns when speaking or listening to others actively. For many ADHD children it's really difficult to listen to others because they are so excited to share their own story as well. It's not that they don't care about the other person, but because they believe their story will connect with the other person. Practicing conversations will help your child to start conversations and engage in meaningful discussions. Through role-playing your child will also learn how to handle challenging social situations, like disagreements. By incorporating roleplaying and social scripts into your parenting approach, you can equip your child with valuable social skills and enhance their ability to navigate social interactions successfully, promoting positive peer relationships and social confidence.

Empathy and Understanding

A big part of being socially successful relies on your ability to be empathetic and understanding toward others. You wouldn't be friends with someone who never understood what you're going through or who wasn't empathetic toward your pain, right? Well, most children struggle with this, not just children with ADHD. However, since kids with ADHD often miss cues sent by their friends, they might come across as unempathetic or as if they don't care. You can help your child to be understanding toward others by embracing empathetic responses, encouraging a change in perspective, and promoting kindness and compassion.

Empathetic Responses

In order to help your child respond to others with empathy, they first need to see it modeled. As parents, you should start by responding to each other, and to your children, with empathy, even when you're feeling frustrated. When your child sees you acting empathetically toward everyone, they will pick up on your behavior and follow your lead. One of the best ways to address empathy as a topic is by discussing the empathy in movie or book characters that they love. For example, Alice had empathy toward the Red Queen in *Alice in Wonderland*, and The Weasleys showed empathy toward Harry in *Harry Potter*. Discussing behavior that is empathetic will help your child to understand what empathy is much more clearly. By understanding what it is and what it looks like within social situations, your child will know how to behave in order to also model empathetic behavior and have empathetic responses. When you see your child showing signs of empathy toward others, be sure to praise their behavior by saying what you appreciate about their behavior. For example, "Thank you for sharing your toys with your sister when she cried. It means a lot to me to see that you understand her sadness and want to make her feel better." By praising and thanking them for the specific behavior, they are more likely to repeat the same type of empathetic behavior in the future.

Encouraging Perspective

The same goes when encouraging your child to have a fresh perspective on things. Talking about how others might perceive things or how they might see certain situations will start to cement the idea in your child that not everyone thinks the way that they do. It will help them to understand that sometimes, they need to try and see things the way that others do. You can encourage your child to have a different perspective by teaching them how to listen to friends and then imagine that they are in their shoes. For example, a while ago my son came home with news that his friend's parents were getting a divorce. "Would you like to make him a card and get him a present?" I asked him. "Why?" he responded, surprised, "It's not something to celebrate." I knew it was the perfect time to encourage taking his friend's perspective. "If it was me and Dad getting a divorce, how would you feel?" I asked gently. "Very sad," he said after a minute of silence. "What would make you feel better if you're sad?" He thought about it before answering, "Eating ice cream and knowing that my friends care about me." I then encouraged him to now imagine what his friend was feeling in that moment and what might cheer him up. "His soccer ball is at his old house and he's staying with his grandparents now. He said that he missed it. I think I should give him my ball and write a note to say that he can always come and play here."

By encouraging a different perspective, they'll start to do it by themselves as well. Eventually, they'll encourage a change of perspective on their own, helping them to be better friends, employees, and even employers.

Kindness and Compassion

Kindness and compassion are something that we should all nurture and it starts at home. We should all foster a culture of kindness at home to emphasize the importance of being compassionate toward each other. For example, you can all volunteer together or decide to help others together as a family. When your children see kindness in action, they'll start to model it themselves. I remember when I was a little girl, we all got ice creams one summer day. As we walked on the beach, my dad's ice cream fell into the sand. I remember thinking, "Thank goodness it's not mine!" Then, I watched as my mom handed her ice cream to my dad. He was reluctant to take it but she insisted. I remember asking her whether she didn't like ice cream, to which she said, "I love ice cream, but I wanted Daddy to have the best day ever." A few weeks later, at a princess-themed birthday party, my friend fell and broke her tiara. In that moment, I remembered my mother's words and handed my friend my tiara. Because I saw kindness in action, it was easy for me to act kindly and with compassion. By promoting empathy, perspective-taking, and kindness, you can nurture your child's emotional intelligence and enhance their ability to build strong and meaningful relationships with others, contributing to their social and emotional growth.

Friendship Building

Building friendships is hard for everyone. That's why every second movie includes a plot where someone struggles to make friends or only has one or two close friends. Building friendships can be even trickier when you are neurodivergent. Luckily, as parents, there are a couple of things that we can do to help our children build healthy friendships. In an earlier chapter, we discussed the power of having playdates to help your child socialize, but now we're taking it a step further.

Inclusive Behavior

It's vital that we teach our children to be inclusive toward others, regardless of how different they might look or behave. Children are generally much better than us adults at this. They tend to focus on what they have in common and not what makes them different from one another. So, the first lesson is for us as parents—to be openminded when it comes to friendships. If your child befriended someone at school that has a different family dynamic, culture, race, or abilities than your child, don't discourage the friendship. When you show inclusive behavior, so will your child. They might not always get it right though, so it's important that you also address it when they aren't acting inclusively. Encourage your children to play with all the friends, even the one alone in the corner that everyone else is making fun of, and then make sure that you're also chatting to all the moms and giving everyone a fair chance. You can model inclusive behavior by

- celebrating diversity and being open to other cultures and races.

- using inclusive language and avoiding stereotypes.

- expanding your own social circle.

- making use of inclusive media and books.

- addressing bias and discrimination when you encounter it.

By incorporating these practices into your daily life, you can effectively model inclusive behavior for your child, shaping their values and influencing their interactions with the diverse world around them.

Playdates and Events

The best way to help your child build friendships is by creating opportunities for them to make friends. Whether you're hosting a playdate or perhaps a sleepover, hosting people will give your child the opportunity to socialize within a safe environment. When hosting events or playdates, make sure that you have activities planned that align with your child's interests, otherwise they might not be interested in socializing with the other people anyway. The more invested they are, the better chance that they'll engage and enjoy talking to others about it. You should also collaborate with other parents by communicating specific needs. If you see that your child is struggling to make friends, reach out to another mom and explain the situation to her, then plan something that you can do together. It's important that your child never feels set-up, or like they're on a blind date. Even if you're going to someone else's house for the sake of your child and theirs to connect, tell your child that you're going to spend time with your friends or to talk about something specific. If your child knows that they're being "set-up," it might be too much pressure for them, causing them to opt out of any conversation.

Friendship Challenges

Your child will inevitably run into some friendship problems. Like all children, at some point, they'll have an argument or fight over a toy (or a girl). It's essential that you're attentive to your child's emotions and feelings when it comes to their friends. Ask them to explain to you what happened without immediately offering advice. Whatever you do, don't rush to conclusions and don't jump on the phone and start threatening other moms. Take a moment to listen and use it as an opportunity to teach your child valuable conflict resolution techniques. Help your child to effectively express their own emotions and also listen to the emotions of their friends. Eventually, things will sort themselves out, so try not to get too involved. Rather, just offer advice and a supportive shoulder to your child.

By encouraging inclusive behaviors, organizing social events, and supporting your child through friendship challenges, you can assist them in developing meaningful and positive peer relationships, fostering a strong sense of belonging and social connection. Now that we have covered how to boost your child's social skills, let's move on to the importance of self-care for parents.

Chapter 10:

Embracing Self-Care

You know those days where everything just goes wrong and you feel like an absolute failure of a human being? Well, a while ago, I had one of those. It started when I overslept because I convinced myself that closing my eyes after turning off my alarm wasn't dangerous. While running 15 minutes late, I burnt my son's toast, which he then refused to eat. My daughter couldn't find her notebook anywhere and my husband had to leave for work before the children were ready for carpooling, so I had to take them to school myself. On the way to school, I realized that we didn't run through our morning checklist and that my son forgot his ENTIRE backpack at home. On top of that, I hit the sidewalk with the car, causing a flat tire, and I screamed at my children to stop fighting so that I could fight with the insurance guy over the phone. Yes, not my proudest moment. It was chaotic, it was madness, and it was exhausting. As I sat on the sidewalk, waiting for my friend to show up and take me home, I burst into tears. "I'm a hamster stuck on a death wheel," I told her through tears, "but if the hamster stops running, her tiny hamster family will die."

What I experienced then was the tip of the iceberg and a couple of weeks later, I was rushed to the emergency room, convinced that I was having a heart attack. Turns out, I wasn't having a heart attack, but I was experiencing something else: burnout and anxiety. I was totally surprised by my diagnosis. I don't have a crazy-stressful job with high stakes. I don't jump out of planes or do things that are generally considered scary. But, I am a mom who would give everything for her children and that fact that you're here, reading up about ADHD, means that you are also a parent or a caregiver that would give it all. Well, as beautiful as that is, it can also be dangerous. That's why you need to embrace self-care for yourself. Surprise—this chapter is about taking care of yourself and not your kids; we'll get back to them later.

Recognizing Parental Stress and Burnout

You know the funniest part of my anxiety and burnout story? I told the doctor he was wrong at least three times. I told him I didn't feel any different than what I usually do and that I was fine. Eventually, he brought me a book from his office; a thick one filled with descriptions of disorders and diseases. He opened up the book to the *Burnout and Stress* section and asked me to read the signs and symptoms out loud. Well, turns out, I was stressed and burned out, I just had no idea what the signs were before. So, let's take a look at the signs and symptoms of burnout to assess where your stress levels are at.

The Signs and Symptoms

As you read through these signs and symptoms, take note of how many might be applicable to you. Burnout and stress share many similar symptoms, as burnout is often a result of prolonged stress. Here's a list of common signs and symptoms of burnout and stress.

Emotional Symptoms

- **Emotional exhaustion:** Feeling drained, overwhelmed, and unable to cope with emotional demands.

- **Detachment:** Feeling emotionally detached from your work, colleagues, or clients.

- **Negativity:** Increased cynicism, pessimism, and negativity toward your work or life in general.

- **Reduced sense of accomplishment:** Feeling like your work is meaningless or unappreciated.

- **Loss of motivation:** Lack of enthusiasm, drive, or ambition.

Physical Symptoms

- **Fatigue:** Feeling tired, exhausted, or lacking energy, even after adequate rest.

- **Sleep problems:** Difficulty falling asleep, staying asleep, or experiencing unrestful sleep.

- **Headaches:** Frequent headaches or migraines.

- **Digestive issues:** Stomachaches, nausea, or other digestive problems.

- **Muscle tension:** Aches, pains, or muscle tension, particularly in the neck, shoulders, and back.

- **Changes in appetite:** Loss of appetite or overeating.

Behavioral symptoms

- **Procrastination:** Putting off tasks or avoiding responsibilities.

- **Increased irritability:** Feeling easily agitated, impatient, or short-tempered.

- **Social withdrawal:** Isolating yourself from friends, family, or social activities.

- **Substance use:** Increased use of alcohol, drugs, or other substances to cope with stress.

Cognitive symptoms

- **Difficulty concentrating:** Trouble focusing, paying attention, or remembering things.

- **Poor decision-making:** Making impulsive or rash decisions.

- **Increased errors:** Making more mistakes or experiencing a decline in work performance.

If you read through this list and it felt more like your own bio than a list of symptoms, it's time to face the music and accept that you might be struggling with some stress and burnout. Now comes the big question: why? In short, because parenting is REALLY hard! If you're not convinced that you need to do something about it though, here's some encouragement. Your mental well-being will have a large impact on your child's development. I know that's a hard pill to swallow but your stress can influence your relationship with your child because when you're extremely irritable, you probably won't want to entertain them as much. Your stress can also lead to an increase in stress for them, since they can sense your frustrations and stress. That's why you need to take care of yourself in order to provide better care for them.

Overcoming Guilt

The reason why most parents don't practice self-care is because they feel like they're being selfish. The guilt that comes with parenting can be overwhelming, especially when you don't allow yourself to catch a breath. You need to begin this journey of self-care by acknowledging that you need help and that it's okay to take a break. I'm not saying book a solo trip to Ibiza and hide there for a month. However, it's okay to eat the last piece of cake or take a bubble bath while the kids watch TV. Or, better yet, why not call a babysitter and go out for dinner? Small pockets of self-care can make a massive difference in your day-to-day life and stress levels. In order to overcome guilt, you also need to start practicing self-compassion. Recognize that parenting is hard and that you're doing the best you can, and stop beating yourself up over the burned cupcakes or the failed baked sale. You deserve to take care of yourself, regardless of your "performance" as a parent. So, start prioritizing self-care by engaging in activities that you like to manage your stress better. By recognizing signs of stress and burnout, understanding the impact on the child's development, and seeking support, you can take proactive steps to maintain your well-being and provide a more stable and nurturing environment for your child with ADHD.

Practicing Self-Care

Self-care is the practice of taking care of one's own physical, mental, and emotional health. It involves engaging in activities that promote well-being and reduce stress. Self-care is essential for everyone, but it is especially important for parents, who often put the needs of their children ahead of their own. For parents, self-care can be challenging, but it is vital for their own well-being and for the well-being of their families. When parents are well-rested, mentally healthy, and emotionally balanced, they are better able to cope with the demands of parenting and provide their children with the love and support they need. Let's have a look at three different ways to implement self-care into your daily routine.

Time Management

Time management is a crucial self-care practice for parents, as it allows them to balance their responsibilities effectively while still making time for their own well-being. Effective time management can help parents reduce stress, increase productivity, and create more time for self-care activities. Here are some practical time management tips for parents:

- **Prioritize and Delegate:** Identify the most important tasks and prioritize them accordingly. Delegate tasks to your partner, children (age-appropriate), or consider outsourcing if possible.

- **Set Time Limits:** Set time limits for tasks to avoid spending too much time on one thing. Use timers or time-tracking apps to stay on track.

- **Utilize Downtime:** Make use of small pockets of downtime throughout the day, such as while commuting or waiting, to tackle small tasks or engage in quick self-care activities.

- **Embrace Flexibility:** Things don't always go according to plan. Be flexible and adjust your schedule as needed. Don't beat yourself up if things don't go perfectly.

- **Schedule Self-Care:** Deliberately schedule time for self-care activities, just as you would schedule any other important task. This ensures you prioritize your well-being.

- **Say No:** Learn to say no to additional commitments that might overburden your schedule. It's okay to prioritize your own well-being and family time.

Self-Care Practices

If you're not sure where to start with practicing self-care, I've got you covered. Here are some self-care practices that parents can incorporate into their daily routines. Remember, self-care doesn't have to be elaborate or take a lot of time. Sometimes a small change can make a big difference.

- **Prioritize Sleep:** Aim for 7-8 hours of quality sleep each night. Establish a regular sleep schedule and create a relaxing bedtime routine.

- **Nourish Your Body:** Eat nutritious meals throughout the day, including plenty of fruits, vegetables, and whole grains. Stay hydrated with water and avoid excessive caffeine or sugary drinks.

- **Incorporate Movement:** Engage in regular physical activity, even if it's just a short walk or some at-home exercises. Find activities you enjoy and make them a part of your routine.

- **Practice Mindfulness:** Take a few minutes each day to practice mindfulness or meditation. Focus on your breath, observe your thoughts without judgment, and cultivate a sense of calm.

- **Connect With Loved Ones:** Make time to connect with friends and family, even if it's just a quick phone call or video chat. Social connections are crucial for emotional well-being.

Hobbies and Interests

As parents, we often push our own hobbies to the back burner. We have cupboards covered in dust with all of the things that we enjoy doing. Part of self-care can be to rediscover your own hobbies and interests and make time to enjoy them. Whether you want to paint or bake, dance or watch TV, it's important that you reconnect with yourself and do things that you enjoy. This includes connecting with your own friends and joining the social world again where you have a community of support. However, if you want to carve out time for yourself, you'll have to set some boundaries so that you get time for the things you want to do amidst all the parenting responsibilities.

By practicing effective time management, implementing self-care practices for mental and emotional well-being, and nurturing hobbies and interests outside of parenting, parents can maintain their well-being and resilience while caring for a child with ADHD, ensuring they have the energy and strength to provide the best support possible.

Building a Supportive Network

No matter how strong you are, you can't go through life alone. You need a supportive network of people who love you and want to see you succeed. Connecting with other parents of children with ADHD can provide invaluable support, understanding, and practical advice. Sharing experiences, strategies, and resources with others who have faced similar challenges can make a significant difference in a parent's journey. A big part of self-care is finding others who you can do life with.

The Benefits of Connecting With Others

Sometimes we just need to know that we're not alone and that there are others who understand us and what we're going through. That's why it's valuable to connect with other parents of children with ADHD. Connecting with other parents is incredibly beneficial in various ways.

- **Shared Understanding and Empathy:** Talking to other parents who understand the unique challenges of raising a child with ADHD can provide a sense of validation and reduce feelings of isolation.

- **Exchange of Strategies and Resources:** Parents can share effective strategies for managing ADHD symptoms, navigating school systems, and advocating for their children's needs.

- **Emotional Support and Encouragement:** Sharing experiences and offering encouragement can help parents feel less alone and more equipped to handle the challenges of raising a child with ADHD.

- **Sense of Community and Belonging:** Connecting with other parents creates a sense of community and belonging, reducing feelings of isolation and providing a safe space to share experiences.

- **Learning from Others' Experiences:** Parents can learn from the experiences of others, gaining insights into different approaches, therapies, and resources that might benefit their child.

Friends and Family

When it comes to support and understanding, don't overlook the friends and family that you already have. Even if they don't have children with ADHD, they can help you through the difficult times and celebrate the good times as well. Having people you can rely on for emotional support, practical assistance, and companionship can help you navigate life's challenges and enhance your overall happiness.

Here are some tips for building a strong support system:

- **Nurture Existing Relationships:** Invest time and energy into your existing relationships with friends and family. Make regular contact, show appreciation, and be there for them when they need you.

- **Be Open and Authentic:** Let people get to know the real you. Share your thoughts, feelings, and experiences openly and honestly. This builds trust and deepens connections.

- **Don't Be Afraid to Ask for Help:** When you need assistance, don't hesitate to reach out to your support network. People are often willing to help if you ask.

- **Maintain Reciprocity:** Relationships are a two-way street. Offer support and assistance to others as well, creating a balanced and mutually beneficial support system.

Remember, building a strong support system takes time and effort. Nurture your connections, be open to new relationships, and don't hesitate to ask for help when needed. A strong support system can make a significant difference in your overall well-being and happiness.

Professional Help

Another way to manage your stress and burnout is by seeking professional help. Even though there is a certain stigma surrounding getting professional help, it is nothing to be ashamed of. In fact, by getting professional help, you are showing your children just how much you love them and that they should take care of their mental well-being as well. Getting professional help doesn't mean that you're failing as a parent, but actually quite the opposite. It means that you're willing to do whatever it takes to help your child with ADHD achieve his or her best life. By connecting with other parents of children with ADHD, building a strong support system of friends and family, and seeking professional help and counseling when needed, parents can create a nurturing and supportive network that empowers them to navigate the parenting journey with confidence and resilience.

Now that we emphasized the importance of self-care, let's start working on family support.

Chapter 11:

It's All About Family

Can I say something brutally honest? Even though I love my son who has ADHD and I wouldn't trade him for the world, parenting him effectively takes a toll on the entire family. I don't blame him for it for one second, but it's the truth and denying it won't change the fact that it's happening. In fact, denying it would probably only place more strain on relationships. There are three relationships that require extra attention and love when you're parenting a child with ADHD. The first relationships that takes strain is the relationship with your partner. Parenting in general can place a lot of pressure on a marriage or a relationship, and even more so when you have to deal with diagnoses and find ways to manage it all. In this chapter, we'll look at how to not only strengthen these relationships, but use them to the advantage of the overall family dynamic. We'll start by looking at parental partnerships, then we'll explore how to manage siblings and ADHD. Finally, we'll look at involving the extended family and how to make sure that no one gives unsolicited advice over Thanksgiving dinner.

Strengthening Parental Partnerships

Building a strong relationship with your partner is crucial for your well-being, as well as for your child's well-being. When there's a united front between parents and caregivers it ensures consistent and effective strategies for managing children's behavior and promoting their overall well-being. By working together, parents can share a deeper understanding of ADHD, collaborate on problem-solving, offer mutual emotional support, and advocate effectively for their child's needs. This collaborative approach creates a supportive environment that helps the child thrive and manage their ADHD symptoms more effectively. All of this offers proof as to why you and your partner need to be united as one.

A United Approach to Parenting

When it comes to parenting, you and your partner need to foster a united front. This requires communication, respect, and a strong commitment toward one another. Here are a couple of practical ways that you can achieve a united front as parents:

- **Prioritize Respectful Dialogue:** Approach discussions with an open mind and a willingness to listen to your partner's perspective. Avoid criticizing or dismissing their views, even if you disagree.

- **Acknowledge Individual Strengths:** Recognize and appreciate each other's strengths as parents. Each partner may bring unique skills or approaches to parenting, which can complement each other.

- **Discuss Differences Privately:** If disagreements arise, address them privately with your partner. Avoid arguing or contradicting each other in front of the children.

- **Compromise and Find Common Ground:** Be willing to compromise and find common ground on parenting decisions. This may involve adjusting expectations or finding a middle ground that both partners can support.

- **Present a United Front to Children:** When communicating with children, present a united front. Support each other's decisions and avoid undermining each other's authority.

The first step to the united approach starts by discussing and aligning discipline strategies, routines, and expectations that you have of your children. After agreeing on these things, you need to regularly check in with one another to ensure consistency in parenting methods and minimize confusion in your children. It can be really confusing for children when Mom says one thing, but Dad allows another. You and your partner need to be on the same page and agree on all methods of discipline. You and your spouse should also prioritize spending quality time together as a couple to maintain a strong bond and reduce the strain that parenting a child with ADHD can bring.

Supporting One Another's Well-Being

Another element of strengthening your partnership includes supporting each other's well-being. First and foremost, you need to acknowledge that you and your partner might have different coping mechanisms and emotional reactions to parenting challenges. While you might find peace in a bathtub filled with bubbles, your partner might just need 30 minutes of uninterrupted television time. By understanding each other's coping mechanisms, you can work together to provide each other with what you each need. As parents and partners, you need to encourage each other to practice self-care and pursue individual hobbies and interests. However, you also have to find the balance in supporting yourself as well as your partner. One great way of doing this is by scheduling alone time every week, where each parent gets the opportunity to do what they want to do while the other parent takes care of the responsibilities. For example, perhaps you want to go golfing each Saturday morning, while your partner wants every Friday night to themselves. You can work together to support each other's well-being, both mentally and physically.

Communicate Openly and Honestly

In order to maintain a strong connection as partners and as parents, you need to embrace open communication. You and your partner need to establish a safe space for communicating, where you get to express your thoughts and concerns without judgment. This should be a space where you can express your feelings about the challenges and successes of parenting a child with ADHD while working together toward solutions. Maintaining open and honest communication with your spouse after having children is crucial for a healthy relationship and a supportive parenting partnership. Here are some strategies to foster open communication:

- **Schedule Regular Check-Ins:** Set aside dedicated time for regular check-ins with your spouse to discuss your feelings, concerns, and needs. This could be a weekly or biweekly date night or a daily conversation after the kids are asleep.

- **Use "I" Statements:** When expressing your own feelings or concerns, use "I" statements instead of accusatory language. For example, say "I feel overwhelmed with household chores" instead of "You never help with cleaning."

- **Avoid Criticism and Blame:** Avoid criticizing or blaming your spouse for their actions or parenting choices. Instead, focus on understanding their perspective and finding solutions together.

- **Acknowledge and Validate Feelings:** Acknowledge and validate your spouse's feelings, even if you don't fully agree with them. This shows that you respect their emotions and are willing to listen.

- **Seek Professional Help if Needed:** If communication challenges persist or you struggle to resolve conflicts effectively, consider seeking professional help from a therapist or counselor specializing in couples counseling.

Remember, open and honest communication is a two-way street. Both partners need to be committed to listening, understanding, and expressing their feelings in a respectful and constructive manner. By prioritizing communication, you can maintain a strong and supportive relationship with your spouse, even as you navigate the challenges of parenthood. However, the relationship between you and your spouse isn't the only one that might take some strain when you have a child with ADHD.

Siblings and ADHD

Recognizing that ADHD in one child can strain sibling relationships is crucial for parents to effectively manage family dynamics and foster healthy interactions between siblings. Having a sibling with ADHD can be challenging, especially when they require additional attention and resources. It can be hard on children to see their siblings get special treatment in various areas, especially when they're still very young. There are three ways that you can help siblings to cope with their ADHD siblings:

- helping them understand

- avoiding rivalry

- involving them in the process

Sibling Understanding

Helping children understand and empathize with siblings who have ADHD can foster stronger sibling relationships, reduce conflict, and create a more supportive family environment. Here are some strategies to promote understanding:

- **Age-Appropriate Explanations:** Provide age-appropriate explanations about ADHD, using simple language and relatable examples. Explain that ADHD affects the brain and makes it harder for their sibling to control certain behaviors or focus on tasks.

- **Highlight Strengths and Challenges:** Emphasize that ADHD is not a character flaw or a reflection of their sibling's personality. Highlight their sibling's strengths and talents while acknowledging the challenges they face due to ADHD.

- **Share Resources and Stories:** Provide age-appropriate books, videos, or online resources that explain ADHD in a relatable way. Share stories of successful individuals with ADHD to demonstrate that it doesn't define a person's potential.

- **Encourage Empathy and Compassion:** Encourage siblings to put themselves in their sibling's shoes and imagine how they might feel when facing challenges. Foster a sense of empathy and compassion for their sibling's struggles.

- **Promote Open Communication:** Encourage siblings to talk openly about their feelings and concerns regarding their sibling's ADHD. Create a safe space for them to express their frustrations and seek solutions together.

Remember, fostering understanding takes time and patience. Continuously educate siblings about ADHD, encourage empathy, and provide support to help them navigate the challenges and build stronger relationships with their sibling who has ADHD.

Avoiding Rivalry

Sibling rivalry can be more pronounced when one sibling has ADHD, as the symptoms of ADHD can lead to disruptive behaviors, impulsivity, and emotional outbursts that may strain the relationship. Here are some strategies to address and avoid sibling rivalry in this situation:

- **Foster Empathy and Acceptance:** Encourage siblings to empathize with their sibling with ADHD. Help them understand that certain behaviors are not intentional and that their sibling may need extra support and understanding.

- **Promote Individual Strengths:** Recognize and celebrate each child's unique strengths and talents. Avoid comparisons and focus on fostering each child's individual growth and development.

- **Provide Individual Attention:** Spend quality time with each child individually. This helps them feel valued and appreciated, reducing feelings of neglect or favoritism.

- **Teach Conflict Resolution Skills:** Teach siblings effective conflict resolution skills, such as active listening, compromise, and respectful communication. Help them navigate disagreements constructively.

Involving Siblings

Siblings don't have to stand on the sideline and watch as their brother or sister with ADHD gets additional support. In fact, oftentimes, children act out or become jealous because they want to be part of the solution and not just a bystander. So, why not involve siblings? Siblings can actually play a significant role in supporting and understanding their sibling with ADHD. Here are some ways they can be involved (Pierce, 2023):

1. **Be a Friend and Confidant:** Offer a listening ear and a safe space for their sibling to express their feelings, frustrations, or concerns. Show empathy and understanding for their challenges.

2. **Provide Gentle Reminders:** Help their sibling stay on track with tasks or routines by offering gentle reminders or prompts. Avoid nagging or criticizing, and instead, offer support and encouragement.

3. **Engage in Shared Activities:** Participate in activities that both siblings enjoy, such as playing games, engaging in hobbies, or spending time outdoors. These shared experiences can strengthen their bond and provide a sense of normalcy.

4. **Offer Help With Organization:** Assist their sibling with organizing their belongings, creating study schedules, or managing their time effectively. This can help reduce stress and improve their sibling's ability to focus.

5. **Practice Patience and Understanding:** Recognize that ADHD can make it difficult for their sibling to control certain behaviors or emotions. Be patient, understanding, and avoid taking their sibling's actions personally.

6. **Advocate for Their Sibling:** Stand up for their sibling if they face bullying or unfair treatment due to their ADHD. Be a supportive voice and advocate for their sibling's needs.

7. **Educate Others About ADHD:** Help educate friends, classmates, or extended family members about ADHD to promote understanding and reduce stigma. Share resources and information about ADHD to foster a more supportive environment for their sibling.

8. **Respect Boundaries and Personal Space:** Recognize that their sibling may need time alone or quiet spaces to recharge. Respect their boundaries and avoid overwhelming them with demands or expectations.

9. **Celebrate Their Successes:** Acknowledge and celebrate their sibling's achievements, big or small. Positive reinforcement can boost their confidence and motivation.

10. **Seek Guidance When Needed:** If siblings feel overwhelmed or struggle to cope with their sibling's ADHD, encourage them to seek guidance from parents, therapists, or counselors. Seeking support is a sign of strength, not weakness.

By actively participating in their sibling's support system, siblings can contribute to a more positive and understanding environment for their sibling with ADHD, fostering stronger sibling bonds and promoting overall family well-being.

Extended Family and Support

When it comes to extended family, things can be a little tricky. While some family members might be interested and supportive, others might not understand all too well. However, extended family plays an important role in helping your child with ADHD live a well-adjusted and supported life, filled with people who have their back. As a parent, there's not much you can do to control your extended family or the things that they say, but you can always educate them and involve them in the journey.

Educate Extended Family Members

Educating extended family members about your child's ADHD is crucial for fostering a supportive and understanding environment that promotes your child's well-being and development. Here's why it's important:

1. **Enhanced Understanding and Empathy:** Educating extended family members helps them understand the challenges your child faces and empathize with their struggles. This can reduce misunderstandings, judgment, and negative interactions.

2. **Consistent Support and Encouragement:** Informed extended family members can provide consistent support and encouragement to your child, reinforcing positive behaviors and promoting their self-esteem.

3. **Reduced Stigma and Misconceptions:** Education helps dispel common misconceptions and stigma surrounding ADHD, creating a more accepting and inclusive environment for your child.

4. **Collaborative Approach to Care:** Informed family members can become active participants in your child's care, offering support, sharing observations, and collaborating with you to ensure your child's needs are met.

To educate extended family members continuously, you can share information and resources with them and provide them with reliable information about ADHD, such as articles, books, or videos. You can also encourage them to ask questions and seek clarification, leading to open communication. By maintaining open communication with extended family, you'll create an opportunity for them to be part of the highs and the lows. It's essential that you also involve them in the treatment. When someone is struggling to understand what ADHD really is and how it affects your child, invite them to attend therapy sessions or doctor's appointments, with your child's consent, to gain deeper insights into their condition and treatment strategies. As a parent, you can also address any misconceptions or outdated beliefs they may have about ADHD in a way that's kind and non-aggressive. Provide evidence-based information and correct any inaccurate statements to help them understand what ADHD really is.

Involving Extended Family

Most family members want to be involved. When they are part of your child's celebrations and failures, they will be less likely to make a snarky remark or speak out of turn. When they are involved, they'll feel a deeper connection with your child and have a better understanding of who they are and what they might be experiencing. Do you remember the story I told you during the introduction of this book about my family members giving unsolicited advice to my son such as, "Just study for longer periods"? Well, one of my aunts in particular didn't understand the "whole ADHD phase" (her words, not mine). I knew I had two options in front of me: be angry and tell her off, or extend kindness and help her to understand that it's more than a phase. So, I invited her to spend the day with me and my son at his favorite restaurant. Instead of trying to explain to her what it means to have ADHD, I gave my son the opportunity to show her. You see, a couple weeks earlier, he had asked me how to explain to someone what

ADHD is. We talked about it, and he wanted to put it into practice. That day, he explained with great patience, compassion, and detail that ADHD isn't a phase, but that it's actually a disorder. He explained the symptoms, gave examples, and even drew her a chart of how his thought process usually worked. I watched with pride as he explained and as she listened. When he was done explaining, he asked whether he could please go and play in the park to get rid of some energy. While he was away, my aunt turned to me and apologized for not understanding. She then offered to drive him to the park every weekend to spend some special time with him. By involving her, she understood more about him than ever before.

By strengthening parental partnerships, fostering understanding among siblings, and engaging extended family and community support, families can create a robust support network that bolsters their ability to navigate the challenges of ADHD parenting while promoting a nurturing and harmonious family environment. Now that we understand how to strengthen your family support group, let's conclude our journey by celebrating progress and embracing the future.

Chapter 12:

Looking to the Future

We've already covered so many great topics in this book, but before we say goodbye to one another, there's one more topic that's absolutely essential to discuss. It's probably something that's been on your mind for quite some time and I wouldn't be surprised if it's the reason you picked up this book in the first place: the future. We're all scared of the future to some extent, but nothing compares to the fear of wondering where your children will end up one day, whether they have ADHD or not. However, when you're in a phase of life where your ADHDer is struggling emotionally, physically, and academically, it can be hard to remain hopeful. In this chapter, we'll put it all out there. We'll talk about the fears and answering that looming question: What now? Now that you have all the information you need, you need to look toward the future and apply the knowledge you've acquired on this journey every single day. As we look to the future, we need to recognize three things:

- We have to start celebrating the progress immediately and stop waiting for "one day."

- We have to embrace the fact that our children have endless potential.

- We have to keep going and keep trying, no matter how hard it is.

Celebrating Growth and Learning

As humans, we tend to wait for BIG events before we celebrate something. We wait until we graduate before we feel accomplished, or we wait until a special day before eating a piece of cake. However, celebrating growth and learning is an essential part of the process, both for yourself and for your child. It helps to reinforce positive behaviors, increase motivation, and build a sense of community. So, don't wait for a major moment before you start celebrating. Do it often, and do it boldly.

Reflecting on Your Child's Progress

The first way that you can celebrate growth is by regularly reflecting on your child's achievements, both big and small. It doesn't have to be academically focused; instead, you can celebrate the fact that they had a successful playdate or learned a new emotional regulation skill. Start by celebrating milestones and progress in managing ADHD symptoms, as well as other ways that they've been succeeding. Remember to use positive reinforcements to make them feel like they're doing something right and achieving something important. You can also teach them to reflect on their own progress by asking them what they're proud of each week.

Acknowledging Parental Growth

The second way that you can celebrate growth and learning is by acknowledging your growth as a parent. Take a moment to recognize and appreciate the efforts and resilience that you've displayed as a parent in supporting your child. Celebrate your own victories and improvements, and take a moment to give yourself and your partner a pat on the back. Be compassionate with yourself and acknowledge that parenting a child with ADHD can be difficult, but that it is also deeply rewarding.

The Transformative Power of the Journey

Finally, celebrate growth and learning by embracing the journey of being a parent to a child with ADHD. See it as an opportunity to grow in yourself and your own knowledge of things. You can choose to either crumble under the pressure, or see setbacks and challenges as opportunities for both you and your child to develop resilience and problem-solving skills. When things feel like they're too much to deal with, remember to find strength in the progress that you've already made and put one foot in front of the other.

By reflecting on your child's progress, acknowledging your growth and resilience as a parent, and embracing the transformative power of the journey, you can foster a positive and supportive environment that celebrates achievements and promotes a strong parent-child bond, ultimately unlocking your child's potential and supporting their success in life.

The Endless Potential of Every Child

Every child with ADHD holds a reservoir of untapped potential, a wellspring of boundless energy and creativity waiting to be channeled into remarkable achievements. Often misunderstood as a hindrance, ADHD can be the very catalyst that propels these extraordinary individuals toward greatness. Their boundless energy can translate into tireless dedication when they find a passion that ignites their spirit. Their minds, often buzzing with a multitude of thoughts, can become powerhouses of innovation, generating groundbreaking ideas that challenge conventional thinking. Their ability to hyperfocus can transform them into masters of their chosen fields, their unwavering attention producing works of exceptional depth and detail.

Embracing Hope and Optimism

Being optimistic and hopeful doesn't mean that you're naive or blind to reality. It simply means that you choose to focus on strengths instead of struggles. Having ADHD doesn't mean that your child will never succeed and it doesn't have to affect their entire identity. When you embrace hope and maintain a positive outlook on life, they won't see having ADHD as something that is holding them back. So, choose to look for success stories and choose to embrace hope and optimism for their sake. The journey of a child with ADHD is not without its challenges, but with the right support and understanding, their unique strengths can shine through, transforming perceived limitations into extraordinary capabilities. Their endless potential, once unleashed, can leave an indelible mark on the world, reminding us that the very traits that set them apart are the ones that can propel them toward greatness. By embracing hope and optimism, understanding the endless potential of children with ADHD, and empowering parents to continue supporting their child's growth, you can create an environment that nurtures your child's strengths and potential, leading to a fulfilling and successful journey through life.

Continued Support

As you look to the future, you should embrace an approach of continued support. Helping your ADHD child become the best version of themselves isn't a one-off thing, but a continuous cycle of support and care. It also means that this probably won't be (and shouldn't be) the last book you read about ADHD. In fact, there are so many helpful resources out there that you can make use of. By continuing the supportive role that you play in your child's life, you can help them to achieve everything they wish to achieve. Even when things feel impossible as you look toward the future right now, remember to also look at the past. Look how far you've come already and the progress your child has made. Now look to the future again and remember that they'll continue to grow, just like you.

Conclusion

I can't believe we're already at the end of this incredible journey. But I have a bit of a surprise for you. You see, this is actually not the end of the journey; it's only the beginning! Now the work begins. Implementing all that you've learned on this journey with me might not come easy and it might be hard and feel impossible at times, but keep going. We have a motto in our home that we live by. When we've had a rough day, we encourage each other by saying, "After the worst day comes the best one." So, dear parent, when you feel like you're at your wits' end, don't give up—the best days are yet to come! Trust me, the first time you see your ADHD child laugh with friends, regulate their emotions in the midst of a crisis, or when they get their first B+ on a test, you'll know that it's all worth it!

I hope that this book has equipped and empowered you with all the tools you need to take your next step in helping your ADHDer. I hope that you feel inspired to try new methods and strategies, and that above all, you feel hopeful for the future. If you still feel overwhelmed, that's totally normal. Take a deep breath and let's recap just how much you've learned on this journey and why you can now confidently continue ahead.

- We started the journey by learning more about the science of ADHD. We got close and comfortable by peeling back the layers of what ADHD is and what it isn't. We addressed misconceptions and set the stage for the rest of the book.

- We looked at different parenting styles and why positive parenting is so helpful and successful when it comes to dealing with ADHD. We talked about positive reinforcements and how to collaborate with teachers and other professionals.

- In Chapter 3, we looked at the different routines that ADHDers need in order to succeed. We discovered what makes a morning routine successful, what should be included in an after-school routine, and why a bedtime routine determines success for the next day.

- We also explored the power of effective communication and how expressing expectations can help both you and your child to better understand one another . We also explored the act of active listening and how to incorporate that into your daily conversations.

- We learned about behavior modification techniques and how to use them to successfully manage hyperactivity and other ADHD symptoms.

- In Chapter 6, we discussed emotional well-being and how we can help our children to be mentally and emotionally healthy and happy. We also discussed teaching our ADHD children how to be emotionally intelligent and why it's essential for them to have good emotional skills.`12

- Next, we explored academic success and how we can help our children to achieve their dreams while being realistic. We looked at what it means to be successful as we explored different learning styles and how to tailor a learning environment specifically for each type of learner.

- Since transitions and changes in life are inevitable, we discussed how to manage change and introduce our ADHDers to transitions to help them feel comfortable and confident.

- We explored the importance of social skills and how we as parents can help our ADHD children to be well-adjusted in the social world and be good friends to others. We also looked at ways to encourage positive friendships without being too involved.

- Chapter 10 was designed for you, the parent, to remind you to take care of yourself and have a break every now and again. We talked about the importance of self-care and how you should embrace taking care of your own well-being in order to help your child do the same thing.

- We discussed different ways that ADHD can impact other relationships, such as marriages, between siblings, and with extended family. We looked at a couple of ways to include other family members to create a stronger bond instead of a sense of separation.

- Finally, we looked toward the future! We now know that the opportunities are endless and that our ADHD children will be happy, healthy, well-adjusted humans as long as we put in the work today.

As you can see, my friend, we've covered a lot of incredible topics on this journey. We discussed ADHD from all sides and that's why I am confident that you are now ready to take what you've learned and apply it to your life. Remember, you're not alone, and with a support system on your side, this knowledge in your mind, and all the love in your heart, nothing will stop you from making a success of this journey with your special ADHDer.

If you've enjoyed this book, please leave a positive review so that together, we can continue to help parents just like you. Now, get out there and have some fun with your ADHD child. I can't wait to hear all your success stories!

Dear Reader,

If you find enjoyment and value in this book, I kindly invite you to consider leaving a review. Knowing that my words have resonated with you and contributed positively to your journey would mean the world to me. It's my genuine aspiration to make a meaningful impact and touch the hearts of as many individuals as possible through my writing.

The process of crafting this book was an absolute joy for me, and it's a delight to share my insights and experiences with you. I'm excited to share that there are many more literary endeavors in progress, each one designed to offer guidance, inspiration, and support on various aspects of life. I'm committed to continuing this journey of exploration and discovery with you.

Your support, by leaving a review, empowers me to continue doing what I love most—creating content that resonates and connects. Your engagement fuels my passion and propels me forward. So, please keep an eye out for upcoming titles, as there's so much more I'm eager to share.

I also wrote a smaller book called **"13 Magical Affirmations for Kids: Embracing the Power Within and Finding Calm in Your Heart"**. It's ment to be used as a tool to calm your child or help sooth them to sleep while boosting their self-esteem whenever they need it. It is a great way to help build bonds between child and parent. Check it out in audible form!

Once again, I extend my heartfelt gratitude for choosing to embark on this reading adventure with me. Your involvement is a testament to the shared bond between authors and readers, and it reinforces my belief that stories have the power to shape lives. I'm genuinely excited to see where this literary journey takes us, and I deeply appreciate your role in making it possible.

Warm Regards,

Regina

If you would like to be a part of Regina's ARC Team (Advanced Readers Copy) please send her a message at **contactme@reginamichaels.com** or visit **ReginaMichaels.com**

References

Behold the magic of a consistent routine. (2016, November 28). ADDitude. https://www.additudemag.com/slideshows/daily-routine-for-adhd-child/

Ben Turkia, I., Brahim, T., & Sahli, L. (2023). Emotional intelligence and attention-deficit/hyperactivity disorder (ADHD). *European Psychiatry,* *66*(S1), S512–S512. https://doi.org/10.1192/j.eurpsy.2023.1087

Brain Balance Centers. (n.d.). *Important insights into ADHD learning styles and other learning disabilities.* Brain Balance Centers. https://www.brainbalancecenters.com/blog/important-insights-into-adhd-learning-styles-and-other-learning-disabilities#:~:text=Physical%20or%20kinesthetic%3A%20With%20this

CDC. (2023, January 23). *Active listening | communicating | essentials | parenting information | CDC.* Centers for Disease Control and Prevention. https://www.cdc.gov/parents/essentials/toddlersandpreschoolers/communication/activelistening.html

Cherry, K. (2023, February 23). *Understanding body language and facial expressions.* Verywell Mind; Verywellmind. https://www.verywellmind.com/understand-body-language-and-facial-expressions-4147228

Duggal, N. (2016, April 5). *Dopamine and attention deficit hyperactivity disorder (ADHD).* Healthline. https://www.healthline.com/health/adhd/adhd-dopamine#connection

Edelman, G. (2006, October 6). *How to make friends: A guide for kids with ADHD (and their parents, too)*. ADDitude; New Hope Media LLC. https://www.additudemag.com/how-to-make-friends-a-guide-for-kids-with-adhd/

Fletcher, J. (2022, June 16). *Mindful listening: What it is and how to practice it*. Psych Central. https://psychcentral.com/lib/mindful-listening-exercise#7-tips-for-mindful-listening

Hasan, S. (2018). *ADHD (for parents)*. Kids Health. https://kidshealth.org/en/parents/adhd.html

Hasan, S. (2022, May). *ADHD for parents*. Kidshealth. https://kidshealth.org/en/parents/adhd.html#:~:text=Kids%20with%20ADHD%20can%20show

Jones, H. (2022, January 17). *Do ADHD symptoms differ in boys and girls?* Verywell Health. https://www.verywellhealth.com/do-adhd-symptoms-differ-in-boys-and-girls-5207995

Low, K. (2019). *Negative ADHD behaviors can impact the social skills of children*. Verywell Mind. https://www.verywellmind.com/how-to-improve-social-skills-in-children-with-adhd-20727

Marie, S. (2021, September 23). *What causes ADHD: Is it nature or nurture?* Healthline. https://www.healthline.com/health/adhd/environmental-causes-of-adhd

Neurodiversity and neurodivergence: A guide for families. (2022, August 15). Raising Children Network. https://raisingchildren.net.au/guides/a-z-health-reference/neurodiversity-neurodivergence-guide-for-families#embracing-neurodiversity-nav-title

Pierce, R. (2023, August 9). *Supporting A sibling with executive functioning challenges: Tips and strategies | life skills advocate*. Life Skills

Advocate. https://lifeskillsadvocate.com/blog/supporting-a-sibling-with-executive-functioning-challenges/#:~:text=It

Roth, E., & Weiss, K. (2021, October 14). *Types of ADHD: Inattentive, hyperactive-impulsive, and more.* Healthline. https://www.healthline.com/health/adhd/three-types-adhd#types

Rudy, L. (2022, January 12). *Autism vs. ADHD: What are the differences?* Verywell Health. https://www.verywellhealth.com/autism-vs-adhd-5213000

Simram. (2022, April 30). *How to fight OCD?* Mantra Care. https://mantracare.org/ocd/ocd-treatment/how-to-fight-ocd/

Thenu, L. (2022, May 8). *Parent education: Confusing ADHD and LD: They are not the same thing!* Foothills Academy. https://www.foothillsacademy.org/community/articles/confusing_adhd_and_ld

University of Washington. (2019). *What is an individualized education plan?* Washington. https://www.washington.edu/accesscomputing/what-individualized-education-plan

Watson, S. (2022, July 13). *Treating adult ADHD: Noradrenergic agents.* WebMD. https://www.webmd.com/add-adhd/adult-adhd-noradrenergic-agents#:~:text=This%20chemical%20helps%20you%20stay

Wilkins, F. (2023, May 2). *How is the ADHD brain different?* Child Mind Institute. https://childmind.org/article/how-is-the-adhd-brain-different/#:~:text=Scientists%20have%20seen%20differences%20in

www.ingramcontent.com/pod-product-compliance
Lightning Source LLC
Chambersburg PA
CBHW060256150626
46553CB00019BA/2415